GO!
with Microsoft®

Office 2010
Discipline Specific Projects

**Shelley Gaskin,
Nancy Meiklejohn, and
Karla Rodie**

Prentice Hall

Boston   Columbus   Indianapolis   New York   San Francisco   Upper Saddle River
Amsterdam   Cape Town   Dubai   London   Madrid   Milan   Munich   Paris   Montreal   Toronto
Delhi   Mexico City   Sao Paulo   Sydney   Hong Kong   Seoul   Singapore   Taipei   Tokyo

Associate VP/Executive Acquisitions Editor, Print: Stephanie Wall
Editorial Project Manager: Laura Burgess
Editor in Chief: Michael Payne
Product Development Manager: Eileen Bien Calabro
Development Editor: Ginny Munroe
Editorial Assistant: Nicole Sam
Director of Marketing: Kate Valentine
Marketing Manager: Tori Olson Alves
Marketing Coordinator: Susan Osterlitz
Marketing Assistant: Darshika Vyas
Senior Managing Editor: Cynthia Zonneveld
Associate Managing Editor: Camille Trentacoste
Production Project Manager: Mike Lackey
Operations Director: Alexis Heydt
Operations Specialist: Natacha Moore

Senior Art Director: Jonathan Boylan
Cover Photo: © Ben Durrant
Text and Cover Designer: Blair Brown
Manager, Cover Visual Research & Permissions: Karen Sanatar
Manager, Rights and Permissions: Zina Arabia
AVP/Director of Online Programs, Media: Richard Keaveny
AVP/Director of Product Development, Media: Lisa Strite
Media Project Manager, Editorial: Alana Coles
Media Project Manager, Production: John Cassar
Full-Service Project Management: PreMediaGlobal
Composition: PreMediaGlobal
Printer/Binder: Quad/Graphics
Cover Printer: Lehigh-Phoenix Color
Text Font: Bookman Light

Credits and acknowledgments borrowed from other sources and reproduced, with permission, in this textbook appear on appropriate page within text.

Microsoft® and Windows® are registered trademarks of the Microsoft Corporation in the U.S.A. and other countries. Screen shots and icons reprinted with permission from the Microsoft Corporation. This book is not sponsored or endorsed by or affiliated with the Microsoft Corporation.

CIP data in file with the Library of Congress.

10 9 8 7 6 5 4 3 2

Prentice Hall
is an imprint of

www.pearsonhighered.com

ISBN 10:   0-13-703753-8
ISBN 13: 978-0-13-703753-7

Contents

Access 2010

Chapter 3 Discipline Specific Assignments.......60

PowerPoint 2010

Chapter 4 Discipline Specific Assignments.......83

About the Authors

Shelley Gaskin, Series Editor, is a professor in the Business and Computer Technology Division at Pasadena City College in Pasadena, California. She holds a bachelor's degree in Business Administration from Robert Morris College (Pennsylvania), a master's degree in Business from Northern Illinois University, and a doctorate in Adult and Community Education from Ball State University. Before joining Pasadena City College, she spent 12 years in the computer industry where she was a systems analyst, sales representative, and Director of Customer Education with Unisys Corporation. She also worked for Ernst & Young on the development of large systems applications for their clients. She has written and developed training materials for custom systems applications in both the public and private sector, and has written and edited numerous computer application textbooks.

This book is dedicated to my students, who inspire me every day.

Nancy Meiklejohn is a Computer Information Systems faculty member and department chair at Pikes Peak Community College. She holds a master's degree in Curriculum and Instruction from the University of Colorado and a bachelor's degree in Business Education from the University of Southern Colorado. She has taught business and information technology courses at Pike's Peak Community College for the past nine years and was named the Colorado Association of Career and Technical Education's Teacher of the Year in 2008. Prior to that, Nancy managed the design, production, and delivery of customized training for a wide variety of business and industry clients.

Karla Rodic has been a Computer Information Systems and Business Technologies faculty member, department chair, and assistant dean at Pikes Peak Community College for 33 years. She recently retired and teaches as an adjunct. She holds a bachelor's degree in Business Education from Colorado State University. She has also developed computer curriculum for business and industry training.

Acknowledgments

Learning is more effective when students understand how course work is related to a career field or higher education. The intent of these projects is to provide students with realistic assignments related to their field of study. We interviewed professionals in their work environments to learn how computer applications are used on the job. The assignments were designed to resemble real-world projects that will engage and challenge students. Students will apply what they learn in the GO! textbook as they complete these projects.

We would like to thank the following professionals in their respective fields for their contributions to our project.

Culinary Arts:

Chef Rob Hudson, CEC, CCE
Department Chair, Culinary Arts Program, Pikes Peak Community College

Chef Peter Aiello, CEC, CEPC
Alpine Chef Catering

Nathan J. Dirnberger, AAS Culinary Arts, AAS Baking & Pastry, AAS Food Service Management
Pikes Peak Community College Culinary Arts Club Founder

Dental Assisting:

Frank Delgresso, BS
Department Chair, Dental Assisting Program, Pikes Peak Community College

Michael Gilbert, DDS
Aspen Dental Associates

Angela Mock, Office Manager
Aspen Dental Associates

Mara Williams, Dental Assistant
Aspen Dental Associates

Susan Silva, EDDA
Aesthetic Dentistry by Design

Fire Science:

Lonnie D. Inzer, MLS
Coordinator of Fire Science and Homeland Security Emergency Management, Pikes Peak Community College

The Men and Women of the Colorado Springs Fire Department

Paralegal:

Michael Adams, JD
Department Chair, Paralegal Program, Pikes Peak Community College

Darla Wildeman, CP
Paralegal, Sparks Willson Borges Brandt & Johnson, PC

Patricia N. Bergeson, CLA, BA, MS Ed
Paralegal, Sparks Willson Borges Brandt & Johnson, PC

We would also like to thank the following people who allowed us to use their smiling faces: Audra Blanch, Ramzy Blanch, Adam Meiklejohn, and Susan Silva.

Discipline-Specific Assignments

You will complete the following discipline-specific projects:

Culinary Arts

Apply the skills from these Objectives:

1. Create a New Document from an Existing Document
2. Change Document and Paragraph Layout
3. Insert and Format Graphics
4. Insert a SmartArt Graphic

GO! Make It | Project **1A** Bistro Letter

Project Files

For Project 1A, you will need the following files:

> w1A_Bistro_Letter
> w1A_Bistro_Logo

You will save your document as:

> Lastname_Firstname_1A_Bistro_Letter

Project Results

Figure 1.1
Project 1A Bistro Letter

(Project 1A Bistro Letter continues on the next page)

GO! Make It | Project 1A Bistro Letter (continued)

Create a new folder to store your Word files in and name the folder **Culinary Arts Word** From the student files that accompany this textbook, locate and open the file **w1A_Bistro_Letter**, and then save the file in the Culinary Arts Word folder as **Lastname_Firstname_1A_Bistro_Letter** Make the following modifications so that the document looks like the one shown in Figure 1.1:

1 Change the top and bottom margins to .5".

2 Insert a page border with a Box setting and a thick outer line/thin inner line. Make the border 3 pt and Purple, Accent 4, Darker 50%.

3 At the top of the page and in the center, from your student files, insert the picture **w1A_Bistro_Logo**. Set the text wrapping to Top and Bottom. Size the picture to 1.2" high by 3.26" wide.

4 Select the first four lines of text beginning with *800 West Pikes Peak Avenue*, and then center it. Reposition the picture so that it is centered above the text.

5 Format the subject line *Gourmet Box Lunches Available for Delivery* as Arial Black font.

6 In the first and last paragraphs of text, apply bold and italic to the *Bistro in a Box* text.

7 In the second blank line below the paragraph beginning *We will make this easy for you*, insert a SmartArt graphic using the Grouped List layout. In the text pane, delete the second bulleted item for each of the three groups. Type the following text in the SmartArt graphic:

www.bistroinabox.com	Online
719-555-1234	Telephone
719-555-1233	Fax

8 Apply the 3D Inset style to the SmartArt graphic and change the colors to Colorful Range – Accent 4 to 5. Size the graphic to 1" high by 6" wide. Under the SmartArt graphic, delete any extra blank lines so that one blank line separates the graphic from the text below it.

9 In the last paragraph, insert a hyperlink on the text *Web site* to the address **http://www.bistroinabox.com**

10 Format the letter by adding blank lines after the subject line, the closing (three blank lines), and the signature line. Compare your document with Figure 1.1 to ensure correct line spacing.

11 Insert a footer with the file name as a Quick Parts field in the left section of the footer.

12 Correct any spelling and grammar errors.

13 Save the document and submit it as directed by your instructor.

 End You have completed Project 1A ———————————

Culinary Arts

Apply the skills from these Objectives:

1. Create a New Document from an Existing Document
2. Change Document and Paragraph Layout
3. Use Special Character and Paragraph Formatting
4. Insert and Format Graphics
5. Create a Table
6. Add Text to a Table
7. Format a Table
8. Create and Modify Lists
9. Set and Modify Tab Stops
10. Insert Footnotes
11. Save a Document as a PDF

GO! Make It | Project **1B** Bistro Form

Project Files

For Project 1B, you will need the following files:

w1B_Bistro_Form
w1B_Bistro_Ribbon
w1B_Bistro_Basket

You will save your documents as:

Lastname_Firstname_1B_Bistro_Form
Lastname_Firstname_1B_Bistro_Form_PDF

Project Results

Figure 1.2
Project 1B Bistro Form

(Project 1B Bistro Form continues on the next page)

Culinary Arts

GO! Make It | Project **1B** Bistro Form (continued)

From the student files that accompany this textbook, locate and open the file **w1B_Bistro_ Form**, and then save the file in the Culinary Arts Word chapter folder as **Lastname_Firstname_ 1B_Bistro_Form** Make the following modifications so that the document looks like the one shown in Figure 1.2:

1 At the top and center of the page, insert the **w1B_Bistro_Ribbon** picture, and then set the text wrapping to In Line with Text. Size the picture to .7" high. Deselect the lock aspect ratio, and then size the picture to 6.6" wide. Apply the color Purple, Accent color 4 Dark; apply the artistic effect Crisscross Etching; and then flip vertical.

2 Convert the title text, *Bistro in a Box*, to WordArt, Gradient Fill – Orange, Accent 6, Inner Shadow. Set the text wrapping to In Line with Text, and then size the title text to .71" high by 3.8" wide. Center the title text. Position the WordArt vertically between the picture and the line containing the text *Order Form*. Add blank lines if necessary to position the text below the WordArt.

3 Center and apply Small Caps formatting to the text *Order Form*. Bold the text, and then increase the font size to 16 pt.

4 On the second blank line below the first paragraph, insert a table with four columns and 11 rows. Type the data in the following tables. Set the width of columns 1 and 3 to 2" wide and columns 2 and 4 to .6" wide. Center the table between the margins. Apply Orange, Accent 6, Darker 25% shading; center and bold the text in cells containing the text *Gourmet Sandwiches, Qty, Specialty Wraps, Qty, Salads,* and *Qty*. Apply Orange, Accent 6, Lighter 60% shading to the unshaded cells in columns 1 and 3. Apply Purple, Accent 4, Lighter 40% shading and bold the text in the last row in the table, row 11. Apply a 2¼ pt top border to row 11.

Gourmet Sandwiches	Qty	Specialty Wraps	Qty
Traditional Club		Florentine Vegetarian	
Southwest Chicken		Asian Delight	
Ham and Cheese Favorite		Beef Chipotle	
Simply Chicken		Chicken Ranchero	
Tasty Turkey			
Rancher's BBQ Beef		Salads	Qty
Italian Hoagie		Chicken Caesar	
Tuna Salad		Cobb Salad	
Pork Tenderloin		Chef's Vegetarian	
TOTAL SANDWICHES		TOTAL WRAPS AND SALADS	

5 As shown in Figure 1.2, apply Wingding bullets to the line beginning with *Free delivery for orders* and the two lines below it and then set line spacing of 12 pt after the first two lines of bulleted text. The third line should be set to 0 pt after.

6 To the right of the bulleted text, insert the **w1B_Bistro_Basket** picture, and then set text wrapping to Behind Text. Apply the Beveled Oval, Black picture style. Size the picture to .9" high by 1.06" wide, and then reposition it so that all bulleted text displays.

7 Insert a bottom paragraph border below the bulleted items. Use a custom setting to create a dashed line that is 2¼ pt thickness, Purple, Accent 4, Darker 50%, as shown in Figure 1.2.

(Project 1B Bistro Form continues on the next page)

GO! Make It | Project **1B** Bistro Form (continued)

8 Center and apply 14 pt Arial Black font to the line containing the text *Call, fax, or visit our Web site to place your order.*

9 On the blank line under *Call, fax, or visit our web site to place your order,* set a left tab at 1.5" and a right tab with dot leaders at 5", and then type the following text:

Phone	719-555-1234
Fax	719-555-1233
Web site	www.bistroinabox.com

10 Insert a footnote at the end of the first paragraph following the text *$9.50 each*. Modify the format of the footnote to use symbols rather than numbers and start with an asterisk. Apply the settings to the footnote, and then insert the footnote text **Prices effective through August 2012**

11 After the second bulleted item *Same day delivery with four hours advance notice,* insert the footnote **Orders for 50 or more lunches require eight hours advance notice**

12 Center the text *Customer Order Information* and apply 12 pt Arial Black font to this text.

13 Convert the five lines of customer information text into a table, separating text at paragraphs. Create the table with one column, and then insert a second column to the right. Format the table using the Light Grid – Accent 4 style. Resize column 1 to 2" wide. Resize column 2 to 4.65" wide. Set the row height to .25" for all rows.

14 Insert a footer with the file name as a Quick Parts field in the right section of the footer.

15 Check the form for spelling and grammar errors and correct any errors you find. Ensure the form fits on one page by removing any extra blank lines if necessary.

16 Save the document. Save the document again as a PDF file with the name **Lastname_Firstname_1B_Bistro_Form_PDF** by selecting PDF in the Save as type list in the Save As dialog box. Submit it as directed by your instructor.

End **You have completed Project 1B** ———————

Culinary Arts

Apply the skills from these Objectives:

1. Create Mailing Labels Using Mail Merge
2. Change Document and Paragraph Layout

GO! Make It | Project **1C** Bistro Labels

Project Files

For Project 1C, you will need the following files:

New blank Word document
w1C_Bistro_Addresses

You will save your document as:

Lastname_Firstname_1C_Bistro_Labels

Project Results

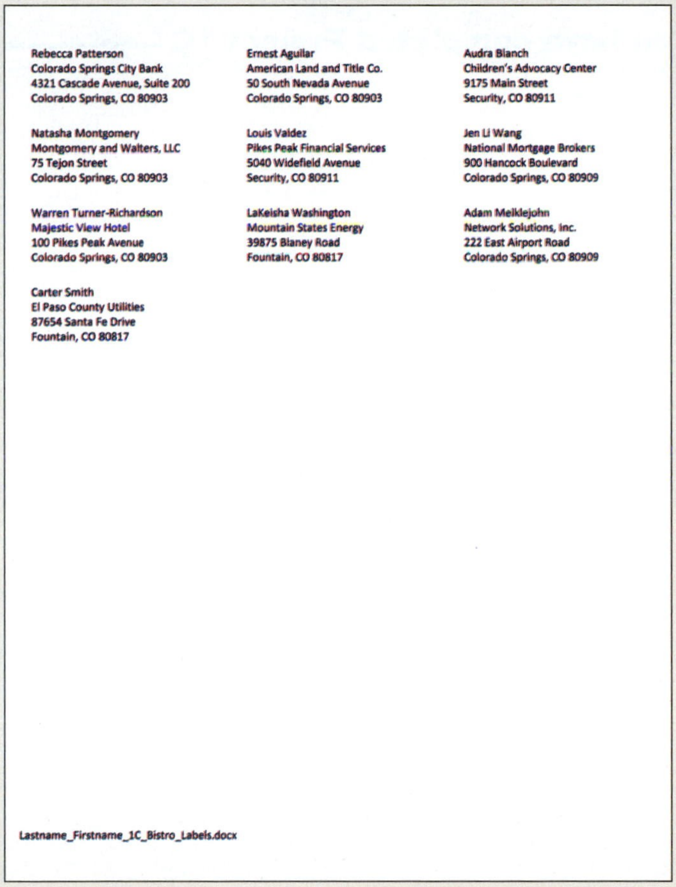

Rebecca Patterson
Colorado Springs City Bank
4321 Cascade Avenue, Suite 200
Colorado Springs, CO 80903

Ernest Aguilar
American Land and Title Co.
50 South Nevada Avenue
Colorado Springs, CO 80903

Audra Blanch
Children's Advocacy Center
9175 Main Street
Security, CO 80911

Natasha Montgomery
Montgomery and Walters, LLC
75 Tejon Street
Colorado Springs, CO 80903

Louis Valdez
Pikes Peak Financial Services
5040 Widefield Avenue
Security, CO 80911

Jen Li Wang
National Mortgage Brokers
900 Hancock Boulevard
Colorado Springs, CO 80909

Warren Turner-Richardson
Majestic View Hotel
100 Pikes Peak Avenue
Colorado Springs, CO 80903

LaKeisha Washington
Mountain States Energy
39875 Blaney Road
Fountain, CO 80817

Adam Meiklejohn
Network Solutions, Inc.
222 East Airport Road
Colorado Springs, CO 80909

Carter Smith
El Paso County Utilities
87654 Santa Fe Drive
Fountain, CO 80817

Lastname_Firstname_1C_Bistro_Labels.docx

Figure 1.3
Project 1C Bistro Labels

(Project 1C Bistro Labels continues on the next page)

GO! Make It | Project **1C** Bistro Labels (continued)

Create a new blank Word document for mailing labels. Save the file in the Culinary Arts Word chapter folder as **Lastname_Firstname_1C_Bistro_Labels** Start the Step by Step Mail Merge Wizard. Set label options to Avery US Letter, 5160 Easy Peel Address labels, and 1" high by 2.63" wide. Browse to select the data source from your student data files **w1C_Bistro_Addresses**. Arrange your labels as Address block and accept the default settings. Update all labels, preview, and then complete the merge.

After the merge is completed, select the document, and then change the spacing to 0 pt before and after paragraphs to ensure that all lines fit in the label area.

Insert a footer with the file name as a Quick Parts field in the left section of the footer. If necessary, delete blank rows at the bottom of the table so that labels will fit on one page.

Save the document and submit it as directed.

 You have completed Project 1C ————————————————————

Apply the skills from these Objectives:

1. Create a New Document from an Existing Document
2. Insert and Format Graphics
3. Change Document and Paragraph Layout
4. Create and Modify Lists
5. Use Special Character and Paragraph Formatting

GO! Think | Project 1D Gala Letter

Project Files

For Project 1D, you will need the following files:

> w1D_PPCC_Logo
> w1D_Gala_Letter

You will save your document as:

> Lastname_Firstname_1D_Gala_Letter

From the student files that accompany this textbook, locate and open the file **w1D_Gala_Letter**, and then save the file in your Culinary Arts Word folder as **Lastname_Firstname_1D_Gala_Letter**

You are the president of the local chapter of the American Culinary Federation. You have been asked to send out a letter to invite local businesses to attend a Chefs' Gala Celebration and fundraising event at a local hotel. The chefs participating are local chefs, and they will cook their favorite menu items to raise money for local charities.

Edit and format a one-page letter inviting local businesses to attend the gala. Add the names of local community organizations and charities in your area that the gala will support. These can include any nonprofit organizations including local food banks, rescue missions, churches, and the American Culinary Education Fund. To complete this assignment, make the following modifications:

1 Create a letterhead with the first three lines in the letter. Convert the words *American Culinary Federation* to a WordArt of your choice. Format the WordArt using WordArt Styles, and then edit the shape with Transform Text Effects. Size the WordArt so it is approximately .78" high and 6.36" wide. Edit text wrapping as needed. Center *Pikes Peak Chapter* horizontally, and then change it to a larger font and small caps. Edit the font color to complement the colors in your WordArt. Center the Web site address horizontally.

2 Insert a page border of your choice.

3 In the top left corner of the page border, insert the **w1D_PPCC_Logo** graphic. Set the text wrapping to Tight. Size the logo so it is approximately 1" high. You may need to adjust the position of the WordArt down on the page so it does nott overlap the graphic.

4 Under the Web site address, insert a bottom paragraph border to separate the letterhead from the text in the letter.

5 Change the text in the letter to Calibri 10 pt.

6 Change the line spacing and paragraph spacing to single spacing with no space before and after the paragraph for the entire letter. Following *August 14, 2012*, insert three blank lines. Following *Sincerely*, insert three blank lines.

7 Insert your own local charities as a list with a customized bullet.

8 Adjust margins and font size appropriately to make sure the letter fits on one page.

9 Add the file name to the left section of the footer as a Quick Parts field.

10 Check the letter for spelling and grammar errors and correct any errors you find.

11 Save the document and submit it as directed.

End You have completed Project 1D

Culinary Arts

1. Create a New Document and Insert Text
2. Insert and Format Graphics
3. Change Document and Paragraph Layout
4. Insert a SmartArt Graphic
5. Create a Table
6. Add Text to a Table
7. Format a Table
8. Use Special Character and Paragraph Formatting
9. Save a Document as a PDF

GO! Think | Project 1E Culinary Gala Flyer

Project Files

For Project 1D, you will need the following file:

New blank Word document

You will save your documents as:

Lastname_Firstname_1E_Gala_Flyer
Lastname_Firstname_1E_Gala_Flyer_PDF

Open a new blank Word document, and then save the file to the Culinary Arts Word chapter folder as **Lastname_Firstname_1E_Gala_Flyer**

In this project, you will create a one-page flyer that explains details about a chef's gala and fundraising event. The flyer will be used to encourage businesses to attend your event. You need to determine information about cost, date, time, reservation information, and menu. Do some research to come up with items for a tempting menu! In addition, you will need to include a list of local charities that will benefit from this event. To complete the assignment, make the following modifications:

1. Add an appropriate title in WordArt. Format the WordArt Shape Style including fill, outline, and effects. Edit text wrapping as needed. Use WordArt Styles to edit the text color, size, and shape.

2. After the title, apply a two-column format, and use both columns to display the flyer information.

3. Use small caps, various font sizes, and various colors throughout the document.

4. Apply paragraph borders and paragraph shading.

5. Include the list of your charities in a table, and then format the table using a design to match other parts of the flyer.

6. Create a text box with the ticket information, and then change the border and shading to match the other colors in the document.

7. Include a SmartArt Picture List to display chef photos and their restaurant names. Search Microsoft Office Clip Art or Office.com to find chef photos to insert in your SmartArt.

8. Use additional Microsoft clip art or photos and apply picture styles throughout the flyer.

9. Add the file name to the right section of the footer using the Quick Parts field.

10. Check the flyer for spelling and grammar errors and correct any errors you find.

11. Save the document and submit it as directed. Save the document again as a PDF file with the name **Lastname_Firstname_1E_Gala_Flyer_PDF** by selecting PDF in the Save as type list in the Save As dialog box and submit it as directed.

End **You have completed Project 1E**

GO! Think | Project 1F Gala Labels

Project Files

For Project 1F, you will need the following files:

New blank Word document
w1F_Gala_Addresses

You will save your document as:

Lastname_Firstname_1F_Gala_Labels

Create a new blank Word document for mailing labels. Save the file in the Culinary Arts Word chapter folder as **Lastname_Firstname_1F_Gala_Labels** Start the Step by Step Mail Merge Wizard. Set label options to Avery US Letter, 5160 Easy Peel Address labels, and 1" high by 2.63" wide. Browse to select the data source from the student data files **w1F_Gala_Addresses**. Arrange your labels as Address block and accept the default settings. Update all labels, preview, and then complete the merge.

After the merge is completed, select the document, and then change the spacing to 0 pt before and after paragraphs to ensure that all lines fit in the label area.

Add the file name to the left section of the footer as a Quick Parts field. If necessary, delete blank rows at the bottom of the table so that the labels fit on one page.

Save the document and submit it as directed.

End **You have completed Project 1F** ―――――――――――――

GO! Make It | Project 1G Dental Newsletter

Project Files

For Project 1G, you will need the following files:

w1G_Dental_Newsletter
w1G_Smiling_Couple
w1G_Smiling_Guy
w1G_Basketball
w1G_Dentist

You will save your documents as:

Lastname_Firstname_1G_Dental_Newsletter
Lastname_Firstname_1G_Dental_Newsletter_PDF

Project Results

Figure 1.4
Project 1G Dental Newsletter

(Project 1G Dental Newsletter continues on the next page)

Dental Assisting

GO! Make It | Project **1G** Dental Newsletter (continued)

Create a new folder to store your Word files and name the folder **Dental Assisting Word** From the student files that accompany this textbook, locate and open the file **w1G_Dental_Newsletter**, and then save the file in your Dental Assisting Word folder as **Lastname_Firstname_1G_Dental_Newsletter** Create a one-page newsletter by modifying the document as shown in Figure 1.4. To complete the newsletter, make the following modifications:

1 Change the bottom margin to .8" and the left/right margins to .5"; leave the top margin at 1".

2 Insert a page border from the Art section of Page Border dialog box as shown in Figure 1.4. Set the width to 10 pt.

3 Convert the title text *Beautiful Smiles* to WordArt style with a Fill - Red Accent 2, Warm Matte Bevel. Change the WordArt text fill to Aqua, Accent 5, Darker 50% and size it to .8" high by 3.76" wide. Set the text wrapping to Top and Bottom. Center the WordArt between the left and right margins.

4 Below the WordArt, insert the **w1G_Smiling_Couple** picture. Set text wrapping to Top and Bottom, and then apply Rounded Diagonal Corner, White picture style. Change the picture border to Aqua, Accent 5, Darker 50%. Size to .8" high by 1.07" wide. Apply picture corrections of Brightness 0% and Contrast +20%. Reposition the picture to the left of the title text.

5 Below the WordArt, insert the **w1G_Smiling_Guy** picture. Set text wrapping to Top and Bottom, and then apply Snip Diagonal Corner, White picture style. Change the picture border to Purple, Accent 4, Darker 50%. Size to .9" high by .81" wide. Reposition the picture to the right of the title text.

6 Below the WordArt, on the first blank line, set a left tab at .5" and a right tab at 7" with preceding dot leaders. At the first tab, type **Published Quarterly by Smiling Families Dental Group** At the second tab, type **April-June, 2012 Edition** Apply bold and italic font styles to the text *Smiling Families Dental Group*.

7 Apply a bottom paragraph border to the line beginning *Published Quarterly* as shown in Figure 1.4. Apply the color Purple, Accent 4, Darker 50%, and then change the width to 3 pt.

8 On the line with the heading *Prepare Your Child for the Appointment*, format the body of the newsletter in two columns with a vertical line between the columns from this point forward.

9 Format the heading *Prepare Your Child for the Appointment* with the font Arial Black 11 pt, and then change the font color to Aqua, Accent 5, Darker 50%. Use the Format Painter to apply these font settings to the other two headings.

10 In the last sentence of the first paragraph, insert a hyperlink to the ADA Web site shown, using the same URL.

11 After the sentence that ends with the word *volleyball* in the *Consider a Mouth Protector* section, insert a footnote that reads **ADA/National High School Athletics Partnership**

12 After the last sentence that ends with the word *child* in the *Consider a Mouth Protector* section, insert a column break.

13 Below the *Consider a Mouth Protector* heading, insert the **w1G_Basketball** picture, and then set the text wrapping to square. Size the picture 1.5" high by 1.5" wide, and then apply a Relaxed Inset bevel picture effect. Position the picture just below the heading text as shown in Figure 1.4.

(Project 1G Dental Newsletter continues on the next page)

GO! Make It | Project 1G Dental Newsletter (continued)

14 Below the *Meet Our New Dentist!* heading, insert the **w1G_Dentist** picture, and then set the text wrapping to square. Size the picture 1.2" high by. 1.19" wide, and then apply the Simple Frame, Black picture style. Position the picture in the middle of the paragraph text at the right margin as shown in Figure 1.4. Delete any blank lines above the *Meet Our New Dentist!* heading.

15 On the blank line below the *Meet Our New Dentist!* section, insert SmartArt using the Converging Radial layout from the Relationship types. Type the following text in the SmartArt and add spaces if necessary to position text, as shown in Figure 1.4:

Office Hours

Monday - Thursday 7:30 a.m. to 5:30 p.m.

Friday 7:30 a.m. to 12:30 p.m.

Weekends Emergencies Only

16 Change the SmartArt colors to Colorful Range - Accent Colors 3 to 4, and then apply the Polished SmartArt style.

17 Near the bottom of the document, convert the office address, phone number, and e-mail information to a table, and then format it in two columns separating text at tabs. Apply the table style Medium Shading 2 - Accent 1. Merge cells, center the text, and then resize columns as shown in Figure 1.4.

18 Insert a footer with the file name as a Quick Parts field in the left section of the footer. In the right section of the footer, insert the text **Printed on Recycled Paper** at the right margin. Move the right tab in the footer to the 7" mark.

19 Check the flyer for spelling and grammar errors and correct the errors you find. Reposition text, objects, and/or remove blank lines so that the document fits on one page.

20 Save the document, and then save the document again as a PDF file with the name **Lastname_Firstname_1G_Dental_Newsletter_PDF** by selecting PDF in the Save as type list in the Save As dialog box. Submit it as directed.

End **You have completed Project 1G** ——————————————

Dental Assisting

Apply the skills from these Objectives:

1 Create a New Document from an Existing Document

2 Insert and Format Graphics

3 Change Document and Paragraph Layout

4 Create a Table

5 Add Text to a Table

6 Format a Table

7 Use Special Character and Paragraph Formatting

GO! Think | Project **1H** Dental Letter

Project Files

For Project 1H, you will need the following file:

   w1H_Dental_Letter

You will save your document as:

   Lastname_Firstname_1H_Dental_ Letter

From the student files that accompany this textbook, locate and open the file **w1H_Dental_Letter**, and then save the file in your Dental Assisting Word folder as **Lastname_Firstname_1H_Dental_Letter**

This letter will be sent to current patients in your dental office to tell them about your new facility. The name of the new office is Colorado Dynamic Dentistry. The address is 2000 W. Broadmoor Bluffs Parkway, Ste. 208, Colorado Springs, CO 80904. The phone number is 719-555-8899, and the Web site is www.dynamicdent.com. To complete the assignment, make the following modifications:

1 Select all of the text in the letter and change the font to Calibri 10 pt.

2 Change the line spacing and paragraph spacing to single spacing with no space before and after the paragraph for the entire letter. Insert three blank lines following *August 14, 2012*. Insert three blank lines following *Sincerely,*.

3 At the top of the letter, create a letterhead for the dental office using the information given for the office. Convert the title of the office *Colorado Dynamic Dentistry* to WordArt. Format the WordArt using WordArt Styles, and then edit the shape with Transform Text Effects. Size the WordArt so it fits across the page.

4 Below the WordArt, edit the font style, size, and color of the address, phone number, and Web site address to complement the WordArt. Insert an appropriate clip art in the letterhead, and then apply picture effects. Below the letterhead information, apply a bottom paragraph border to separate the letterhead from the text in the letter. Format the paragraph border to match the colors in the WordArt.

5 Search the Internet to determine what new procedures and/or technology you will offer. Add that information to the end of the third paragraph.

6 Create a table at the bottom of the letter that shows the hours of operation for the office. The office is open six days per week, Monday through Thursday from 8:30 a.m. to 6 p.m. and 8:30 a.m. to 3 p.m. on Friday and Saturday. Include information that the office offers same-day appointments.

7 Use appropriate margins so the letter fits on one page.

8 Insert the file name in the center section of the footer as a Quick Parts field.

9 Check your document for spelling and grammar errors and correct any errors you find.

10 Save your document and submit it as directed.

 You have completed Project 1H ————————————

Dental Assisting

Apply the skills from these Objectives:

1. Create Mailing Labels Using Mail Merge
2. Change Document and Paragraph Layout

GO! Think | Project 1I Dental Labels

Project Files

For Project 1I, you will need the following files:

New blank Word document
w1I_Dental_Addresses

You will save your document as:

Lastname_Firstname_1I_Dental_Labels

Create a new blank Word document for mailing labels. Save the file in the Dental Assisting Word folder as **Lastname_Firstname_1I_Dental_Labels** Start the Step by Step Mail Merge Wizard. Set label options to Avery US Letter, 5160 Easy Peel Address labels, and 1" high by 2.63" wide. Browse to select the data source **w1I_Dental_Addresses**. Arrange your labels as Address block and accept the default settings. Update all labels, preview, and then complete the merge.

After the merge is completed, select the document, and then change the spacing to 0 pt before and after paragraphs to ensure that all lines fit in the label area.

Add the file name to the left section of the footer as a Quick Parts field. If necessary, delete blank rows at the bottom of the table so that the labels fit on one page.

Save the document and submit it as directed.

End **You have completed Project 1I** ─────────────────────

Dental Assisting

Apply the skills from these Objectives:

1 Insert and Format Graphics

2 Insert and Modify Text Boxes and Shapes

3 Change Document and Paragraph Layout

4 Create a Table

5 Add Text to a Table

6 Format a Table

7 Use Special Character and Paragraph Formatting

8 Save a Document as a PDF

GO! Think | Project 1J Dentist Flyer

Project Files

For Project 1J, you will need the following file:

New blank Word document

You will save your documents as:

Lastname_Firstname_1J_Dental_Flyer
Lastname_Firstname_1J_Dental_Flyer_PDF

Open a new blank Word document. Save the document in the Dental Assisting Word folder as **Lastname_Firstname_1J_Dental_Flyer**

Create a flyer that will be used as a marketing tool to give details about the opening of a new dental practice and services offered at the practice. Include the dentists' qualifications and procedures offered. The name of the new office is Colorado Dynamic Dentistry. The address is 2000 W. Broadmoor Bluffs Parkway, Ste. 208, Colorado Springs, CO 80904. The phone number is 719-555-8899. The office Web site address is www.dynamicdent.com. Make the following modifications to the document:

1 Create a heading for the flyer using WordArt at the top of the flyer. Add an appropriate title in WordArt. Format the WordArt Shape Style including fill, outline, and effects. Edit text wrapping as needed. Use WordArt Styles to edit the text color, size, and shape.

2 Below the WordArt, include the address, phone number, and Web site address. Format this information to complement the colors you used in the WordArt.

3 Use a table to display information about dental procedures offered. Use the Internet to determine what services this practice will offer. Format the table using a design to match the other colors in the flyer.

4 Use a SmartArt Picture List graphic to display information about the dentists. Search Microsoft Office clip art to find dental photos. Include the photos and qualifications in the SmartArt.

5 Add a page border to the flyer.

6 Create a text box, and then list the hours of the practice. Format the borders and shading of the text box to match other items in the flyer.

7 Add other clip art and/or photos that add interest to the flyer, and then apply picture effects.

8 Include a Web site hyperlink.

9 Insert the file name in the center section of the footer using a Quick Parts field.

10 Check your document for spelling and grammar errors and correct any errors you find.

11 Save the document. Save the document again as a PDF file **Lastname_Firstname_1J_Dental_Flyer_PDF** by selecting PDF in the Save as type list in the Save As dialog box. Submit it as directed.

 You have completed Project 1J ⎯⎯⎯⎯⎯⎯⎯⎯⎯⎯⎯⎯

Apply the skills from these Objectives:

1. Create a New Document from an Existing Document
2. Insert and Format Graphics
3. Insert and Modify Text Boxes and Shapes
4. Change Document and Paragraph Layout
5. Create and Modify Lists
6. Insert a SmartArt Graphic
7. Create a Table
8. Add Text to a Table
9. Format a Table
10. Format a Multiple-Column Newsletter
11. Save a Document as a PDF

GO! Make It | Project 1K Fire Station Newsletter

Project Files

For Project 1K, you will need the following files:

w1K_Firestation_Newsletter
w1K_Fire_Border
w1K_Station_8
w1K_Ladder
w1K_Canyon_Fire
w1K_Campfire
w1K_Swift_Water
w1K_CPR
w1K_CSFD_Logo

You will save your documents as:

Lastname_Firstname_1K_Firestation_Newsletter
Lastname_Firstname_1K_Firestation_Newsletter_PDF

Project Results

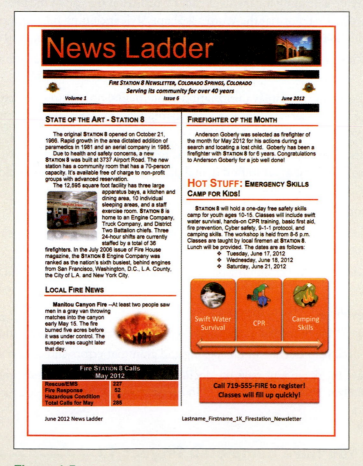

Figure 1.5
Project 1K Fire Station Newsletter

(Project 1K Fire Station Newsletter continues on the next page)

Fire Science

GO! Make It | Project **1K** Fire Station Newsletter (continued)

Create a new folder to store your Word documents and name it **Fire Science Word** From the student files that accompany this textbook, locate and open the file **w1K_Firestation_Newsletter**, and then save the file in your Fire Science Word folder as **Lastname_Firstname_1K_Firestation_ Newsletter** Create the newsletter shown in Figure 1.5 by making the following modifications:

1 Change the top and bottom margins to .4", and then change the left and right margins to .8". Click Ignore if a dialog box opens stating that one or more margins are outside the printable area of the page.

2 Change the font size of the title text *News Ladder* to 52 pt. Change the font color to Gradient fill, Preset, Fire. Insert a 2¼ pt red box paragraph border around the title text. Add black shading. To the right of the title text, insert the **w1K_Station_8** photo. Size the photo to .9" high by 1.15" wide. Set the text wrapping to In Front of Text. Apply the Soft Edge Rectangle picture style. Position the photo at the right edge of the paragraph border.

3 Below the title, leave one blank line, and then insert **w1K_Fire_Border** graphic and size it to look like horizontal lines in the newsletter heading. Size the line approximately .2" by 7".

4 Under the horizontal fire line, center **Fire Station 8 Newsletter, Colorado Springs, Colorado** in Calibri 12 pt bold, italic, and small caps. In the next line, center **Serving its community for over 40 years** in Calibri 12 pt bold and italic.

5 In the next line, use the Tab key to position the text as shown, and then type **Volume 1** Format the text Calibri 10 pt bold and italic. Type **Issue 6** and then format it Calibri 10 pt bold and italic. Type **June 2012** and then format it Calibri 10 pt bold and italic.

6 At the left of *Volume 1*, insert the **w1K_CSFD_Logo** graphic in the letterhead. Size the logo to approximately .34" high by .4" wide. Set the text wrapping to Tight. Edit the logo using Corrections, and then Sharpen by 50%. Copy and paste the logo to the right of the letterhead, and then position it at the right side of the newsletter masthead.

7 Copy and paste the fire border line below the text *Volume 1*. Ensure the size is still .2" high by 7" wide. Your newsletter masthead should look like the top of the newsletter shown in Figure 1.5.

8 At the top of the first column beginning with *State of the Art*, apply a two-column text format with .3" between columns and a line between the columns. Be sure to select *This Point Forward* so the columns are turned on after the heading.

9 Format the first heading *State of the Art - Station 8* to Arial 14 pt bold, small caps, and then add a 2¼ pt red bottom border. Change the paragraph spacing for the first heading to 12 pt before and 10 pt after. Use the Format Painter to copy this format to the other three headings, *Local Fire News*, *Firefighter of the Month*, and *Hot Stuff: Emergency Skills Camp for Kids!*

10 In the first article in the first column, insert the **w1K_Ladder** graphic at the beginning of the third paragraph that begins *The 12,595*. Size it to .95" high by 1.27" wide. Change the text wrapping to Tight. Apply the Reflected Rounded Rectangle picture style. Position the graphic so it is at the left edge of the left column as shown in the figure.

11 In the second article in the first column, insert the **w1K_Canyon_Fire** graphic at the right side of the *Manitou Canyon Fire* article. Size it to 1" high by 1.5" wide. Change the text wrapping to Tight. Apply the Soft Edge Oval picture style. Position the graphic as shown.

(Project 1K Fire Station Newsletter continues on the next page)

GO! Make It | Project **1K** Fire Station Newsletter (continued)

12 Use the Convert Text to Table feature to create a table with the *Fire Station 8 Calls May 2012* information. Create two columns, and then separate text at tabs. Merge the title row, and then center the text. Insert a return after *Calls* to move *May 2012* to the next line. Apply the orange Dark List - Accent 6 table style. Leave the title text white. Size both lines in the title row text to 12 pt. Format the text for the columns black and bold.

13 Immediately before the line *Firefighter of the Month*, insert a column break so the heading is positioned at the top of the second column even with the heading for the first column.

14 In the second column, for three camp dates, insert the custom bullet from Wingdings.

15 In the heading in the second column, format the text *Hot Stuff:* 20 pt Standard Red.

16 At the end of the second column, leave a blank line, and then insert a Continuous Picture List SmartArt graphic to display the three camp topics. Change the color of the SmartArt to Colored Fill - Accent 6 to match the newsletter. Change the SmartArt Style to Best Match for Document, Intense Effect. Size the SmartArt 1.9" high by 3.5" wide. In the first column of the SmartArt, insert the **w1K_Swift_Water** graphic. In the second column, insert the **w1K_CPR** graphic, and then in the third column, insert the **w1K_Campfire** graphic. Add the text **Swift Water Survival CPR** and **Camping Skills** to each shape in the SmartArt.

17 At the bottom of the second column, below the SmartArt, draw a text box, and then apply the Moderate Effect - Orange, Accent 6. Add a 3 pt red border to the text box. Insert and center the text **Call 719-555-FIRE to register!** On the next line, insert and center **Classes will fill up quickly!** Change the text color to 14 pt black and bold. Format the paragraph single spacing with 0 pt before and after the paragraphs. Size the textbox .6" high by 3" wide. Position the text box so it is in the center of the column and approximately even with the bottom of the table in the left-hand column.

18 Search for 5 acres and replace it with **five** acres.

19 Apply a red 3 pt single page border.

20 In the left section of the footer, insert **June 2012 News Ladder** In the right section of the footer, insert the file name using a Quick Parts field.

21 Check the newsletter for spelling and grammar errors and correct any errors you find.

22 Save your completed document. Save your newsletter again as a PDF file **Lastname_Firstname_1K_Firestation_Newletter_PDF** by selecting PDF in the Save as type list in the Save As dialog box. Submit it as directed.

End **You have completed Project 1K** ——————————

Fire Science

GO! Think | Project 1L Fire Science Report

Project Files

For Project 1L, there are no student files.

You will save your document as:

Lastname_Firstname_1L_FireScience_Report

You are a firefighter at a station in your local area. When you are not out on calls, one of your duties is to research topics related to firefighting and fire safety and summarize what you learn in a report. Some good sources of information include www.firesafety.gov, www.usfa.dhs.gov, and www.nfpa.org. Search for and explore other sites related to firefighting. Use the skills you have practiced in this chapter to compose and format a multiple-page report on a topic of your choice related to the fire science field. Open a new blank Word document. Save the document in the Fire Science Word folder as **Lastname_Firstname_1L_FireScience_Report** and then incorporate the following in your report:

1. Format the report in MLA format.
2. Cite at least three sources using MLA format, and then create a bibliography on the last page.
3. Use at least two different fonts.
4. Apply bullets or numbering to a list.
5. Insert and apply effects to at least one photo; use photos found in Microsoft Office.
6. Create a header or footer and include page numbering.
7. Create a table to display data visually.
8. Insert at least one footnote.
9. Use SmartArt appropriately to display information.
10. Make the document two to three pages in length.
11. Add the file name as a footer.
12. Check the document for spelling and grammar errors and correct any errors you find.
13. Save the document. Submit it as directed.

End You have completed Project 1L ———————————————

Apply the skills from these Objectives:

1. Create a New Document from an Existing Document
2. Change Document and Paragraph Layout
3. Use Special Character and Paragraph Formatting
4. Insert and Format Graphics
5. Insert a SmartArt Graphic

GO! Make It | Project **1M** Client Letter

Project Files

For Project 1M, you will need the following files:

w1M_Client_Letter
w1M_Flag

You will save your document as:

Lastname_Firstname_1M_Client_Letter

Project Results

Figure 1.6
Project 1M Client Letter

(Project 1M Client Letter continues on the next page)

GO! Make It | Project **1M** Client Letter (continued)

Create a new folder to store your Word files, and then name the folder **Paralegal Word** From the student files that accompany this textbook, locate and open the file **w1M_Client_Letter**, and then save the file in your Paralegal Word folder as **Lastname_Firstname_1M_Client_Letter** Make the following modifications so that the document looks like the one shown in Figure 1.6:

1 Change the top margin to .5".

2 Right-align the first seven lines of text.

3 Convert the firm name *Trusty, Loyal, & True, LLC* to WordArt Style Gradient Fill – Blue, Accent 1 and size it 1.3" high by 3" wide. Change the text fill to the standard color, Dark Blue, and then apply the Bevel, Circle effect. Set text wrapping to In Front of Text. Position the WordArt at the top of the page at the left margin.

4 Insert the **w1M_Flag** picture, and then set the text wrapping to In Front of Text. Size the picture .85" high by 1.28" wide, and then position it between the firm name and the address. Apply the Soft Edges 5 pt picture effect.

5 On the line containing the e-mail address, apply a bottom paragraph border. Set the style to a thin/thick/thin line, change the color to Dark Blue, and then change the width to 3 pt.

6 Format the letter by adding blank lines between the date, the client address, the salutation, the body of the letter, the signature line, and the word *Enclosure*. Refer to Figure 1.6 for correct line spacing.

7 On the second blank line after the sentence *The time frame for processing this motion is listed below*, insert a SmartArt graphic using the Segmented process layout. In the text pane, delete unneeded sub-bullets. Type the four lines of text below as shown in Figure 1.6.

Prepare Motion for Absentee Testimony—March 17, 2012

Receive Signed Motion from Client—March 27, 2012

File Motion in District Court—April 1, 2012

Take Absentee Testimony—December 15, 2012

8 Change the SmartArt colors to Colorful - Accent Colors, and then apply the Inset style. Set text wrapping to Top and Bottom, size the graphic 2" wide by 4.75" high, and then center it between the left and right margins.

9 Insert a footer with the file name as a Quick Parts field in the left section of the footer. Change footer font if necessary to match the body of the letter.

10 Check your document for spelling and grammar errors and correct any errors you find.

11 Save your document and submit it as directed.

End **You have completed Project 1M** _____

Track Changes

Microsoft Word's Track Changes feature is used in **Project 1N Motion Testimony**. Track Changes is a feature of Word that enables you to view revisions to a document and insert personal comments. This is useful when you are making proposed changes to a document that will later be reviewed by you or others. The changes can be either accepted or rejected. Changes to legal documents are often tracked in this way. For example, a contract might be reviewed by an attorney who will recommend changes. If the changes to the electronic document are tracked, both the original text and the recommended text can be viewed for easy comparison. You can accept or reject changes individually, or you can accept or reject all changes in a document at once.

To track changes while you edit, follow these steps:

1 Open the document that you want to revise.

2 On the **Review tab**, in the **Tracking group**, click the **Track Changes** button. Compare your screen to Figure 1.7.

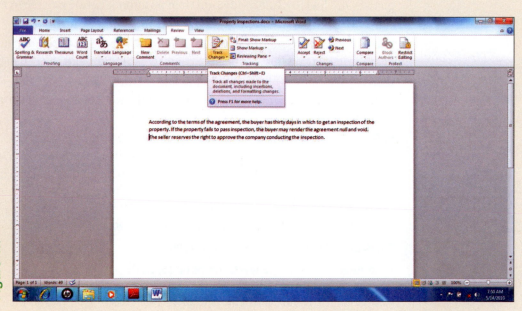

Figure 1.7

(Project Track Changes continues on the next page)

Track Changes (continued)

3 As you edit the document, the text will be marked with a specific color, underline, or strikethrough. Comments are often inserted when changes are tracked, as shown in Figure 1.8. To insert a Comment, position the insertion on the text, and in the **Comments group**, click the **New Comment** button.

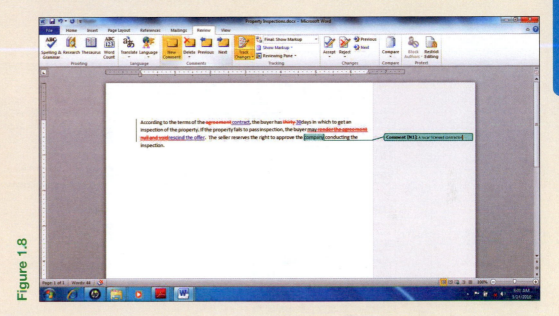

Figure 1.8

4 To turn off the tracking feature, click the **Track Changes** button.

To view changes in a document:

1 Open the document you want to review.

2 On the **Review tab**, in the **Tracking group**, click **Final Showing Markup arrow** to select how the changes are displayed. Compare your screen to Figure 1.9.

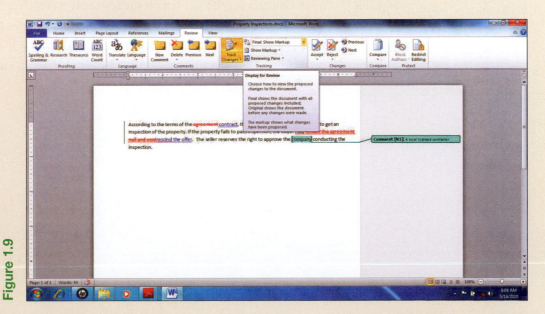

Figure 1.9

(Project Track Changes continues on the next page)

Track Changes (continued)

The Show Markup menu will allow you to customize the way the tracking elements display in your document. Another viewing option is to display the Reviewing Pane as shown in Figure 1.10. To display the Reviewing pane, follow these steps:

1 On the Review tab, in the Tracking group, click the down arrow to the right of Reviewing Pane.

2 Click Reviewing Pane Vertical.

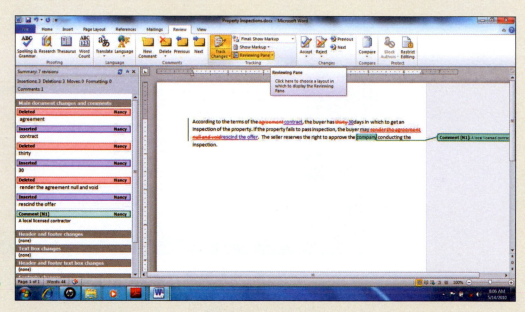

Figure 1.10

To view and accept or reject changes, follow these steps:

1 Open the document you want to review. Place the insertion point at the beginning of the document or at the location where you will begin reviewing changes.

2 Click the **Track Changes** button to turn off the feature if it is active.

3 On the **Review tab**, in the **Changes group**, click **Next** to move to the first change.

4 On the **Review tab**, in the **Changes group**, click the **Accept** button if you want to accept the change. If you want to reject the change, click the **Reject** button. To view another change, click **Previous** or **Next**.

(Project Track Changes continues on the next page)

Track Changes (continued)

5 Click the **Accept button arrow**, and then if you want to accept all of the changes at once, click **Accept All Changes in Document**. Click the **Reject button arrow**, and then if you want to reject all changes at once, click **Reject All Changes in Document**. The default settings accept or reject the change and move on to the next change automatically. See Figure 1.11.

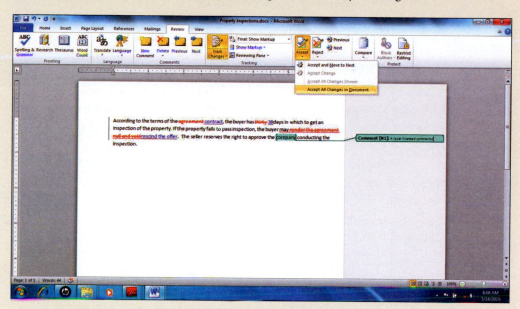

Figure 1.11

To delete the comments any reviewers of the document inserted, right-click on the comment, and then click **Delete Comment**.

Apply the skills from these Objectives:

1. Create a New Document from an Existing Document
2. Edit a Document Using Track Changes
3. Create a Table
4. Change and Reorganize Text
5. Create and Modify Lists
6. Insert Footnotes
7. Use Special Character and Paragraph Formatting
8. Save a Document as a PDF

GO! Make It | Project **1N** Motion Testimony

Project Files

For Project 1N, you will need the following file:

   w1N_Motion_Testimony

You will save your documents as:

   Lastname_Firstname_1N_Motion_Testimony
   Lastname_Firstname_1N_Motion_Testimony_PDF

Project Results

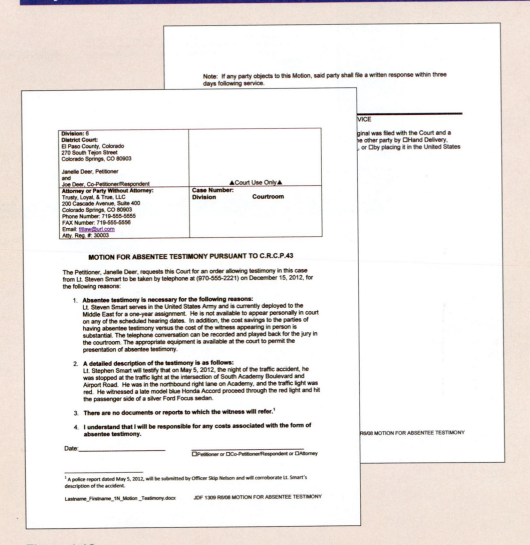

Figure 1.12
Project 1N Motion Testimony

(Project 1N Motion Testimony continues on the next page)

Paralegal

GO! Make It | Project **1N** Motion Testimony (continued)

This project will use the Track Changes feature found on the Review tab of the Ribbon. The **w1N_Motion_Testimony** document was revised with the Track Changes feature turned on. The revisions in the document indicate deleted text and text that has been inserted. This feature is often used in law firms where it is important to track and display proposed revisions to legal documents.

From the student files that accompany this textbook, locate and open the file **w1N_Motion_ Testimony**, and then save the file in your Paralegal Word folder as **Lastname_Firstname_1N_ Motion_Testimony** Create the document shown in Figure 1.12 by modifying the document as follows:

1 Accept or reject the changes marked in this document using the Track Changes feature of Word. Make sure the Display for Review is set to Final: Show Markup and deselect Track Changes if it is enabled. At the beginning of the document, accept and reject changes as follows so that your document matches Figure 1.12.

- Reject the deletion of the phone number *2221*.
- Reject the addition of the phone number *1222*.
- Accept adding the full words *United* and *States*.
- Accept adding the sentence *The appropriate equipment is available at the court to permit the presentation of absentee testimony.*
- Accept adding the words *South* and *northbound*.
- Reject deleting the word *blue* and *reject* adding the words *dark green*.
- Accept deleting *3* and adding *three*.
- Reject deleting *United States* and adding *US*. Click OK.

2 At the beginning of the document, insert a table with two columns and two rows.

3 In the first column, in the first row of the table, type the following text in Arial 10 pt font:

Division: 6
District Court:
El Paso County, Colorado
270 South Tejon Street
Colorado Springs, CO 80903

Janelle Deer, Petitioner
and
Joe Deer, Co-Petitioner/Respondent

4 In the first column, in the second row of the table, type the following text in Arial 10 pt font:

Attorney or Party Without Attorney:
Trusty, Loyal, & True, LLC
200 Cascade Avenue, Suite 400
Colorado Springs, CO 80903
Phone Number: 719-555-5555
FAX Number: 719-555-5556
E-mail: tltlaw@url.com
Atty. Reg. #: 30003

(Project 1N Motion Testimony continues on the next page)

GO! Make It | Project **1N** Motion Testimony (continued)

5 In the first and second rows of the table, bold the text *Division:*, *District Court:*, and *Attorney or Party Without Attorney:*. Add a blank line before *Janelle Deer, Petitioner*.

6 In the second column, in the first row of the table, type the text **Court Use Only** in Arial 11 pt font. Insert a triangle symbol from Wingdings 3 before and after this text. Apply bottom center alignment to the cell to position the text as shown in Figure 1.12.

7 In the second column, in the second row of the table, type the following text in bold Arial 11 pt font. Use Ctrl+Tab to position the text *Courtroom* as shown in Figure 1.12.

Case Number:

Division Courtroom

8 Bold and center the text *Motion for Absentee Testimony Pursuant to C.R.C.P.43*, and then change the font to uppercase Arial 12 pt.

9 Beginning with *The Petitioner, Janelle Deer* to the end of the document, change the font to Arial 11 pt on all text.

10 Find all instances of the word *Stephen* and replace it with **Steven**

11 Apply numbering to the paragraph beginning *Absentee testimony is necessary for the following reasons:* and the three paragraphs that follow it. Format the text as shown in Figure 1.12. Bold the first sentence in each of these four numbered paragraphs.

12 At the end of numbered paragraph 3, insert a footnote that reads **A police report dated May 5, 2012, will be submitted by Officer Skip Nelson and will corroborate Lt. Smart's description of the accident.**

13 Insert a top paragraph border 3 pt above the text *CERTIFICATE OF SERVICE*.

14 Center the text *CERTIFICATE OF SERVICE*.

15 Insert a footer with the file name as a Quick Parts field in the left section of the footer. In the right section of the footer, insert the text **JDF 1309 R6/08 MOTION FOR ABSENTEE TESTIMONY** Change the font size of the footer text to Arial 9 pt.

16 Change the font size of the text *Petitioner or Co-Petitioner/Respondent or Attorney* below the signature line on page 1 to Arial 9 pt.

17 Insert three check box symbols to the left of each of the words *Petitioner*, *Co-Petitioner/Respondent*, and *Attorney* below the signature line on page as shown in Figure 1.12.

18 Insert this same check box symbol in the *CERTIFICATE OF SERVICE* section on page 2 to the left of each of the words *Hand Delivery*, *E-filed*, *Faxed*, and *by placing*.

19 If necessary, add or delete blank lines so that formatting matches that shown in Figure 1.12. Proofread the document for spelling and grammar errors and correct any errors you find.

20 Save the document, and then save the document as a PDF file with the name **Lastname_Firstname_1N_Motion_Testimony_PDF** by selecting PDF in the Save as type list in the Save As dialog box. Submit it as directed.

End **You have completed Project 1N**

Apply the skills from
these Objectives:

1. Create Mailing
Labels Using Mail
Merge
2. Change Document
and Paragraph
Layout

GO! Make It | Project 1O Labels

Project Files

For Project 1O, you will need the following files:

New blank Word document
w1O_Legal_Addresses

You will save your document as:

Lastname_Firstname_1O_Legal_Labels

Project Results

Rebecca Patterson
Colorado Springs City Bank
4321 Cascade Avenue, Suite 200
Colorado Springs, CO 80903

Ernest Aguilar
American Land and Title Co.
50 South Nevada Avenue
Colorado Springs, CO 80903

Audra Blanch
Children's Advocacy Center
9175 Main Street
Security, CO 80911

Natasha Montgomery
Montgomery and Walters, LLC
75 Tejon Street
Colorado Springs, CO 80903

Louis Valdez
Pikes Peak Financial Services
5040 Widefield Avenue
Security, CO 80911

Jen Li Wang
National Mortgage Brokers
900 Hancock Boulevard
Colorado Springs, CO 80909

Warren Turner-Richardson
Majestic View Hotel
100 Pikes Peak Avenue
Colorado Springs, CO 80903

LaKeisha Washington
Mountain States Energy
39875 Blaney Road
Fountain, CO 80817

Adam Meiklejohn
Network Solutions, Inc.
222 East Airport Road
Colorado Springs, CO 80909

Carter Smith
El Paso County Utilities
87654 Santa Fe Drive
Fountain, CO 80817

Lastname_Firstname_1O_Legal_Addresses.docx

Figure 1.13
Project 1O Labels

(Project 1O Labels continues on the next page)

GO! Make It | Project **10** Labels (continued)

Create a new blank Word document for mailing labels. Save the file in the Paralegal Word folder as **Lastname_Firstname_10_Legal_Labels** Start the Step by Step Mail Merge Wizard. Set label options to Avery US Letter, 5160 Easy Peel Address labels, and 1" by 2.63". Browse to select the data source **w10_Legal_Addresses**. Arrange your labels as Address block, and then accept the default settings. Update all labels, and then complete the merge.

After the merge is completed, select the table containing the label data, and then change the spacing to 0 pt before and after paragraphs to ensure that all lines will fit in the label area.

Insert a footer with the file name as a Quick Parts field in the left section of the footer. If necessary, delete blank rows at the bottom of the table so that the labels will fit on one page.

Save the document and submit it as directed.

End **You have completed Project 10** ————————————————

Paralegal

Apply the skills from these Objectives:

1. Create a New Document from an Existing Document
2. Insert and Format Graphics
3. Change Document and Paragraph Layout
4. Change and Modify Lists
5. Use Special Character and Paragraph Formatting

GO! Think | Project **1P** Stock Letter

Project Files

For Project 1P, you will need the following file:

   w1P_Stock_Letter

You will save your document as:

   Lastname_Firstname_1P_Stock_Letter

From the student files that accompany this textbook, locate and open the file **w1P_Stock_Letter**, and then save the file in your Paralegal Word folder as **Lastname_Firstname_1P_Stock_Letter** To complete this letter, make the following modifications:

1 Select all the text in the letter and change the font to Cambria 12 pt. Format the text as single spacing with 0 pt before and after the paragraphs.

2 Insert three blank lines after the date at the top of the letter. Insert three blank lines after *Sincerely,* and then insert your name as the Chief Executive Officer.

3 At the top of the letter, create a letterhead for your law firm. Do a search on the Internet for funny law firm names and pick one for your law firm. Display the name of the firm in WordArt. Format the WordArt using WordArt Styles, and then edit the shape with Transform Text Effects. Size the WordArt so it fits across the page.

4 Below the WordArt, add an address, city, state, ZIP code, and phone number. Edit the font, style, size, and color of this information to complement the WordArt. Insert an appropriate clip art in the letterhead, and then apply picture effects. Below the letterhead information, apply a bottom paragraph border to separate the letterhead from the text in the letter. Format the paragraph border to match a color in the WordArt.

5 Insert custom bullets for the three documents listed, and then indent those items.

6 Insert a page border.

7 If necessary, adjust the margins to make the letter fit on one page.

8 Insert the file name in the center section of the footer as a Quick Parts field.

9 Check the document for spelling and grammar errors and correct any errors you find.

10 Save the document and submit it as directed.

End **You have completed Project 1P** ————————————

GO! Think | Project **1Q** Stock Receipt

Project Files

For Project 1Q, you will need the following files:

> New blank Word document
> w1Q_Stock_Receipt

You will save your document as:

> Lastname_Firstname_1Q_Stock_Receipt

In this project, you will format a return receipt that will be enclosed with letters to stockholders. Stockholders are asked to acknowledge receipt of original stock certificates by signing the receipt and returning it in a return mailer.

Open a new blank Word document and make the following modifications:

1 Change the top and bottom margins to .8".

2 On the first line, type **All About Stock Company** Center the text, and then apply 18 pt bold. Change the font to a color of your choice.

3 On the next line, type **Receipt Acknowledgement** Center the text, and then apply 14 pt bold. Change the font to a color of your choice.

4 Add a bottom border to the line below *Receipt Acknowledgement*.

5 Below the line, insert text from the file **w1Q_Stock_Receipt**. Format the inserted text italic.

6 In the last paragraph that begins *Return this certificate*, apply a paragraph border and shading. Change the font to 14 pt bold small caps. Horizontally center the paragraph. Ensure the text is easy to read. If necessary, change the text color to make it more readable.

7 Copy and paste the entire certificate to the bottom of the page so there are two certificates on one page. Adjust the spacing so the two forms fill up the page.

8 Search Microsoft Office Clip Art or Office.com for legal graphics. In the certificate at the top of the page, insert an appropriate graphic to the left of the line *Receipt Acknowledgement*. Change the wrapping to Tight, and then size the graphic to fit. Copy the graphic to the right of *Receipt Acknowledgment*. Change the wrapping to In Front of Text, and then size the graphic.

9 Copy and paste the graphics to the bottom certificate. Change wrapping to In Front of Text.

10 Ensure that the two certificates are spaced so that the page can be cut in half.

11 Add the file name to the center section of the footer as a Quick Parts field.

12 Check your document for spelling and grammar errors and correct any errors you find.

13 Save the document in your Paralegal Word folder as **Lastname_Firstname_1Q_Stock_Receipt** and submit it as directed.

End You have completed Project 1Q —————————

Paralegal

Apply the skills from these Objectives:

1. Create Mailing Labels Using Mail Merge

2. Change Document and Paragraph Layout

GO! Think | Project 1R Stock Labels

Project Files

For Project 1R, you will need the following files:

New blank Word document
w1R_Stock_Addresses

You will save your document as:

Lastname_Firstname_1R_Stock_Labels

Open a new blank Word document for mailing labels. Save the file in the Paralegal Word folder as **Lastname_Firstname_1R_Stock_Labels** Start the Step by Step Mail Merge Wizard. Set label options to Avery US Letter, 5160 Easy Peel Address labels, and 1" high by 2.63" wide. Browse to select the data source **w1R_Stock_Addresses**. Arrange your labels as Address block, and then accept the default settings. Update all of the labels, and then complete the merge.

After the merge is completed, select the document containing the label data, and then change the spacing to 0 pt before and after paragraphs to ensure that all lines will fit in the label area.

Add the file name to the center section of the footer as a Quick Parts field. If necessary, delete blank rows at the bottom of the table so that the labels will fit on one page.

Save the document and submit it as directed.

 You have completed Project 1R ————————————————

Apply the skills from these Objectives:

1. Create a New Document from an Existing Document
2. Insert and Format Graphics
3. Change Document and Paragraph Layout
4. Format a Table
5. Use Special Character and Paragraph Formatting
6. Save a Document as a PDF

GO! Think | Project 1S Legal Timetable

Project Files

For Project 1S, you will need the following files:

> w1S_Legal_Timetable
> w1S_Legal_Data

You will save your documents as:

> Lastname_Firstname_1S_Legal_Timetable
> Lastname_Firstname_1S_Legal_Timetable_PDF

From the student files that accompany this textbook, locate and open the file **w1S_Legal_Timetable**. Save the file in your Paralegal Word folder as **Lastname_Firstname_1S_Legal_Timetable**

Your law firm uses a Case Management Timetable to follow cases and make sure all deadlines are met. You have been asked to modify the timetable to make it more attractive on the page. Make the following modifications:

1. Change the top, bottom, left, and right margins to 0.8".

2. Convert the title to a WordArt of your choice. Format the WordArt Shape Style including fill, outline, effects, and text wrapping. Edit the text color, size, and shape. Size the WordArt so there is space to the left and right of the WordArt for a graphic.

3. Search Microsoft Office Clip Art or Office.com for legal graphics. At the top of the page, insert an appropriate graphic to the left of the title. Change the wrapping to Tight, and then size the graphic to fit nicely with the WordArt. Copy the graphic to the right of the WordArt.

4. Format the text *Client* and *Matter* to Calibri 12 pt bold small caps. Adjust the underline line length if necessary.

5. From the student files that accompany this textbook, locate the file **w1S_Legal_Data**, and then insert the text into the new document below the *Matter* line. Format the text *A. Pre-Filing Checklist* as Calibri 14 pt bold. Apply a paragraph border and shading of your choice to that text. Use a border and shading that complement the WordArt colors.

6. To the left of *Yes*, insert a check box, and to the left of *No,* in the line that begins with *1,* insert a check box. Use the Tab key to align the *Yes No* check boxes in line A and lines 2-4.

7. Use Format Painter to copy the format from *A. Pre-Filing Checklist* to *B. Pre-Trial Dates* and *C. Post-Trial Setting Dates*.

8. Select the table in *Section B*, and then apply an appropriate table style. Make sure the text is readable and the style is appropriate for the table information. Apply the same table style to the table in *Section C*.

9. Format the footnote as Calibri 10 pt.

10. Add the file name to the center section of the footer as a Quick Parts field.

11. Add a page border to match the colors in the WordArt, borders, and shading.

12. Check the document for spelling and grammar errors and correct any errors you find.

13. Save the document. Save the document again as a PDF file **Lastname_Firstname_1S_Legal_Timetable_PDF** by selecting PDF in the Save as type list in the Save As dialog box. Submit it as directed.

 You have completed Project 1S ————————

Discipline-Specific Assignments

You will complete the following discipline-specific projects:

CULINARY ARTS

GO! Make It | Project 2A Food Costing (p. 38)
GO! Think | Project 2B Hudson Grill (p. 41)

DENTAL ASSISTING

GO! Make It | Project 2C Dental Invoice (p. 43)
GO! Think | Project 2D Dental Order (p. 46)

FIRE SCIENCE

GO! Make It | Project 2E Chow Spreadsheet (p. 48)
GO! Think | Project 2F Station Staffing (p. 53)

PARALEGAL

GO! Make It | Project 2G Stockholder Ledger (p. 55)
GO! Think | Project 2H Billable Hours (p. 58)

Culinary Arts

GO! Make It | Project **2A** Food Costing

Apply the skills from these Objectives:

1. Enter Data in a Worksheet
2. Format Cells with Merge & Center and Cell Styles
3. Chart Data with a Column Chart
4. Check Spelling in a Worksheet
5. Construct Formulas for Mathematical Operations
6. Edit Values in a Worksheet
7. Format a Worksheet
8. Use the SUM, AVERAGE, MIN, and MAX Functions
9. Navigate a Workbook and Rename Worksheets
10. Edit and Format Multiple Worksheets at the Same Time
11. Create a Summary Sheet

Project Files

For Project 2A, you will need the following files:

> e2A_Food_Costing
> e2A_Bistro_Logo

You will save your workbook as:

> Lastname_Firstname_2A_Food_Costing

Project Results

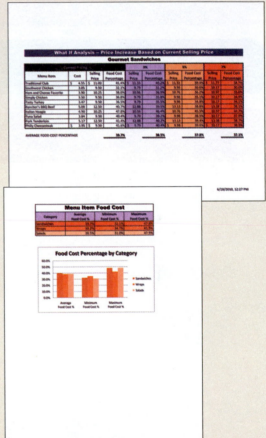

Figure 2.1
Project 2A Food Costing

(Project 2A Food Costing continues on the next page)

Culinary Arts

GO! Make It | Project **2A** Food Costing (continued)

Create a new folder to store your Excel files in, and then name the folder **Culinary Arts Excel** From the student files that accompany this textbook, locate and open the file **e2A_Food_Costing**, and then save the file in your Culinary Arts Excel folder as **Lastname_Firstname_2A_Food_Costing** In the workbook, follow these steps to modify the worksheets as shown in Figure 2.1:

1 Group Sheet 1, Sheet 2, and Sheet 3, and then modify the group as follows:

- Change the top margins to 2", and then center the data horizontally on the page.
- Delete blank rows above and below Bistro in a Box.
- In the center section of the header, insert the file **e2A_Bistro_Logo**.
- In the left section of the footer, insert the code for the file name, and then in the right section of the footer, insert the codes for the current date and time.
- Merge and center cells A1:D1; change the font to Arial Black 18 pt; apply Fill Color Purple Accent 4, Darker 50%; and then change the font color to White, Background 1.
- Merge and center cells A2:D2; change the font to Arial Black 14 pt; and then apply Fill Color Purple Accent 4, Lighter 40%. Autofit rows 1 and 2.
- In cells A3:D3, apply bold, apply middle and center alignment, and then wrap text. Change the row height to 43 pixels.
- In cell A3, insert the text **Menu Item**
- In column A, AutoFit the text.
- In cell D4, insert a formula to calculate the percentage that the cost is of the selling price. Copy the formula to cells D5 through D13. Format cells D4:D13 with Percent Style with one decimal place. Compare your screen to Figure 2.1.
- In cells B4, C4, B13, and C13, format the dollar amounts with Accounting with two decimal places; format the range B5:C12 with Comma Style with two decimal places.
- In cells C15:C17, right-align the text.
- In cells D15:D17, use the Average, Minimum, and Maximum functions to calculate these percentages.
- Apply a bottom border to the cells in row 13.

2 Ungroup the worksheets and rename Sheet1 **Sandwiches** and then apply Tab Color Purple, Accent 4, Darker 25%. Rename Sheet 2 **Wraps** and then apply Tab Color Orange, Accent 6, Darker 25%. Rename Sheet 3 **Salads** and then apply Tab Color Blue, Accent 1, Darker 25%.

3 Rename Sheet4 **Summary**

4 Modify and format the Summary worksheet as follows:

- Merge and center cells A1:D1, and then change the font to Arial Black 16 pt. Autofit row 1.
- For cells A2:D2, bold the text, middle and center align the text, and then apply wrap text. Apply Fill Color Purple, Accent 4, Lighter 60%.
- In row 2, change the row height to 40 pixels. In cells B2, C2, and D2, use the keyboard command [Alt] + [Enter] after the words *Average*, *Minimum*, and *Maximum* to create two lines.
- For columns A, B, C, and D, change the column width to 145 pixels.
- In cells B3:D5, insert cell references from the Sandwiches, Wraps, and Salads worksheets to display the average, minimum, and maximum food cost percentages for the three categories, as shown in Figure 2.1. Apply Percent Style with one decimal place.

(Project 2A Food Costing continues on the next page)

Culinary Arts

GO! Make It | Project **2A** Food Costing (continued)

- For cells A3:D3, apply Fill Color Orange, Accent 6, Darker 25%. For cells A4:D4, apply Fill Color Orange, Accent 6. For cells A5:D5, apply Fill Color Orange, Accent 6, Lighter 60%.

- For cells A1:D5, apply All Borders.

- Insert a Clustered Cylinder column chart to visually display the data in cell range A2:D5. Size and position the chart directly below the data on the same sheet as shown in Figure 2.1. Apply Chart Layout 1 and Chart Style 8 to the chart, and then change *Chart Title* to **Food Cost Percentage by Category**

- Center the data horizontally on the page.

5 On the Sandwiches worksheet, change the selling price of the Rancher's BBQ Beef and Pork Tenderloin to **$12.50** each. Note the changes to the figures on this worksheet and also the Summary worksheet.

6 Modify and format the What If worksheet as follows:

- Change the orientation to Landscape.

- Merge and center cells A1:J1, change the font to Arial Black 14 pt, apply Fill Color Purple Accent 4, Darker 50%, and then change the font color to White, Background 1.

- Merge and center cells A2:J2, and then change the font to Arial Black 14 pt.

- In cell E5, insert a formula to calculate a new Selling Price based on the percentage increase in cell E3 by using absolute cell referencing. Use the fill handle to copy the formula to cells E6:E14.

- In cell F5, calculate a new Food Cost Percentage based on the current cost and the new selling price. Use the fill handle to copy the formula to cells F6:F14.

- Using the skills you practiced, calculate a Selling Price in cells G5 and I5 and a Food Cost Percentage in cells H5 and J5. Hint: Use the current selling price as the base when calculating the increased selling price in cells G5 and I5. Use the current cost as the base when calculating the percentages in cells H5 and J5. Use the fill handle to copy the formulas to cells G6:J14. In column D, right-align the percentages.

- In cells E5:J14, apply Accounting format to rows 5 and 14 in the appropriate cells. Apply Comma Style with two decimals to rows 6–13 where appropriate. Apply Percent Style with one decimal to columns D, F, H, and J.

- In cell A3, apply Black, Text 1 Fill Color, and then change the font color to White, Background 1. In cells E3:F14, apply Fill Color Purple, Accent 4, Lighter 60%, and then apply a thick box border. In cells G3:H14, apply Fill Color Orange, Accent 6, Lighter 40%, and then apply a thick box border. In cells I3:J14, apply Fill Color Orange, Accent 6, Darker 25%, and then apply a thick box border. In cells A3:D14, apply a thick box border.

- In cells F16, H16, and J16, insert the average function to display the Average Food Cost Percentage for each price increase. Apply bold and a bottom double border to those cells. Adjust column width and row height if necessary so that all data is visible.

7 Check the worksheets for spelling and grammar errors and correct any errors you find. Save the workbook and submit it as directed.

End You have completed Project 2A

Culinary Arts

Apply the skills from these Objectives:

1 Enter Data in a Worksheet

2 Construct and Copy Formulas and Use the SUM Function

3 Format Cells with Merge & Center and Cell Styles

4 Chart Data to Create a Column Chart

5 Check Spelling in a Worksheet

6 Construct Formulas for Mathematical Operations

7 Edit Values in a Worksheet

8 Format a Worksheet

9 Use the SUM, AVERAGE, MEDIAN, MIN, and MAX Functions

10 Navigate a Workbook and Rename Worksheets

11 Edit and Format Multiple Worksheets at the Same Time

12 Create a Summary Sheet

GO! Think | Project 2B Hudson Grill

Project Files

For Project 2B, you will need the following file:

  e2B_Hudson_Grill

You will save your workbook as:

  Lastname_Firstname_2B_Hudson_Grill

Open the file **e2B_Hudson_Grill**, and then save it in the Culinary Arts Excel folder as **Lastname_Firstname_2B_Hudson_Grill**

1 Group Sheet 1, Sheet 2, and Sheet 3, and then modify the group as follows:

- Change the orientation to Landscape.
- Center the worksheet horizontally and vertically on the page. Set gridlines to print.
- In row 1, merge and center cells A1:G1. Increase the font size, and then apply bold. If necessary, change the row height to accommodate the text.
- In row 2, merge and center cells A2:G2. Increase the font size, and then apply bold. Change the row height to accommodate the text if necessary. Use Format Painter to copy the format from row 2 to rows 3, 4, and 5.
- For cells A1:A5, apply a fill color of your choice. Make sure the text is readable.
- In the center section of the header, insert the code for the file name.
- For cells C6:E6, apply text wrapping.
- For cells A6:G6, apply bold and center the cells. Apply a top and thick bottom border. Size column A as 300 pixels, and then size columns B through G as 125 pixels.
- Center cells C7:C31.
- In cell B7, apply Accounting format. For cells B8:B31, apply Comma Style.
- In cell D7, insert a formula to calculate total food cost using the cost per item and plates purchased. Use the fill handle to copy the formula to cells D8:D31 for each menu item. In cell D7, apply Accounting format. For cells D8:D31, apply Comma Style.
- In cell B33, insert a formula to calculate the total number of plates purchased. Apply Comma Style with no decimal places. For cells A33:B33, apply bold and a fill color of your choice.
- In cell E7, insert a formula to calculate the percentage of total plates purchased for each menu item using the total plates purchased as an absolute cell reference. Use the fill handle to copy the formula to cells E8:E31 for each item. For cells E7:E31, apply Percent Style with two decimal places.
- In cell B34, insert a formula to calculate the total cost of goods sold for food only based on the SUM of the total food cost. For cells A34:B34, apply bold and a fill color of your choice.
- In cell F7, apply Accounting format. For cells F8:F31, apply Comma Style.

(Project 2B Hudson Grill continues on the next page)

GO! Think | Project **2B** Hudson Grill (continued)

- In cell G7, insert a formula to calculate the total sales for the first item based on the item menu price and the plates purchased. Use the fill handle to copy the formula down to cells G8:G31 for each item. In cell G7, apply Accounting format. For cells G8:G31, apply Comma Style.

- In cell B35, insert a formula to calculate the total sales using the SUM function. For cells A35:B35, apply bold and a fill color of your choice.

- In cell B36, insert a formula to calculate the total profit on food by subtracting the total cost of goods sold from the total sales. For cells A36:B36, apply bold and a fill color of your choice.

2 Ungroup the worksheets.

- Rename the first three sheets according to the month and year in cell A5 of each sheet. Rename the fourth sheet **1st Qtr Summary**

- In the January 2012 worksheet, insert clip art to the left of the title in cell A1. Search for a restaurant clip art or photo in Microsoft Office Clipart. Size the clip art so it fits within rows 1-5. Position the clip art so it is centered between the edge of the sheet and the title. Copy the clip art to the Clipboard. Paste the graphic to the February and March worksheets in approximately the same position.

- In the 1st Qtr Summary worksheet, merge and center cells A1:D1. Increase the font size and add a fill color of your choice. Merge and center cells A2:D2. Increase the font size and add a fill color of your choice. Use Format Painter to copy the format from row 2 to row 3, row 4, and row 5. Adjust the row height if necessary to ensure that all the text is visible.

- In row 6, center the column headings and apply another fill color.

- Create the summary using cell references for the items listed for each month. Center the summary horizontally on the page. For cells A7:D10, add a fill color. For cells B7:D7, apply Comma Style with no decimal places.

- In cell D13, insert a text box, and then type **Highlight Profit** in the box. Ensure that all the text in the box is visible and the text box does not overlap column D. Add a fill color to the box. Draw an arrow from the text box to the March profit to show that March had the highest profit. In the center section of the footer, add the sheet name using the code. Set the Print Area in Page Layout to ensure that the table is horizontally centered.

- Create a chart that shows the First Quarter Summary and includes the information cells A6:D6 and cells A8:D10 for each month. Move the chart to a separate sheet, and then name the sheet **1st Qtr Chart** Apply a style and layout. Add a chart title and horizontal and vertical axis titles. Change the fonts to ensure readability.

3 Check the worksheets for spelling and grammar errors and correct any errors you find. Save the workbook and submit it as directed.

 You have completed Project 2B ——————————————————————

Dental Assisting

1 Enter Data in a
Worksheet

2 Construct and Copy
Formulas and Use
the SUM Function

3 Format Cells with
Merge & Center and
Cell Styles

4 Chart Data to
Create a Column
Chart

5 Check Spelling in a
Worksheet

6 Construct Formulas
for Mathematical
Operations

7 Edit Values in a
Worksheet

8 Format a Worksheet

9 Use the SUM,
AVERAGE, MEDIAN,
MIN, and MAX
Functions

10 Navigate a
Workbook and
Rename Worksheets

11 Edit and Format
Multiple Worksheets
at the Same Time

12 Create a Summary
Sheet

GO! Make It | Project **2C** Dental Invoice

Project Files

For Project 2C, you will need the following files:

e2C_Dental_Invoice
e2C_Smile

You will save your workbook as:

Lastname_Firstname_2C_Dental_Invoice

Project Results

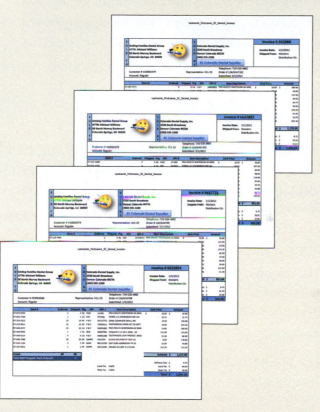

Figure 2.2
Project 2C Dental Invoice

(Project 2C Dental Invoice continues on the next page)

Dental Assisting

GO! Make It | Project **2C** Dental Invoice (continued)

Create a new folder to store your Excel files in, and then name the folder **Dental Assisting Excel** From the student files that accompany this textbook, locate and open the file **e2C_Dental_Invoice**, and then save the file in your Dental Assisting Excel folder as **Lastname_Firstname_2C_Dental_Invoice** In the workbook, follow these steps to modify the worksheets as shown in Figure 2.2:

1 Group Sheet 1, Sheet 2, Sheet 3, and Sheet 4, and then make the following modifications:

- Set the orientation to Landscape.
- Set the top margin to 1.25". Set the left and right margins to .45" and the bottom margin to .5". Center the data horizontally on the page.
- In the center section of the header, insert the code for the file name.
- In cells B2:B5, change the text to Calibri 11 pt, and then apply bold.
- In cells F2:F5, change the text to Calibri 11 pt, and then apply bold.
- In cell I1, change the text to Calibri 16 pt, and then apply bold. Apply a Dark Blue, Text 2, Lighter 60% fill.
- Merge and center cells D9:G9.
- In cells J3:J4, apply bold.
- In cells A1:A7, apply a Blue, Accent 1, Lighter 60% fill, and then apply bold.
- In cells E1:E7 apply a Blue, Accent 1, Lighter 60% fill, and then apply bold.
- In cells A12:K12, apply a Dark Blue, Text 2, Lighter 60% fill, and then center and bold the column headings.
- Center cells C13:D22.
- In cells A24:D24, apply a Blue, Accent 1, Lighter 60% fill, and then apply bold.
- In cells A25:D25, apply a Blue, Accent 1, Darker 25% fill, and then change the text color to white and apply bold.
- In cells I24:K24, apply a Blue, Accent 1, Lighter 60% fill, and then apply bold.

2 Ungroup the worksheets.

- In worksheet 1, in cell F6 in the Sold By section, insert WordArt. Use Gradient Fill – Blue, Accent 1. Change the font to 14 pt. Insert the text **#1 Colorado Dental Supplier** Format the shape style Subtle Effect – Blue, Accent 1. Size the WordArt .3" high by 2.5" wide. Position the upper left corner of the WordArt in cell F6. Copy the WordArt to the Clipboard. Paste the WordArt in to worksheets 2, 3, and 4 at approximately the same position as worksheet 1.
- In worksheet 1, in cell C2, insert the **e2C_Smile** picture. Size the picture .7" high by .98" wide. Apply the Drop Shadow Rectangle picture style. Copy the graphic to the Clipboard. In cell C2 of worksheets 2, 3, and 4, paste the graphic to each sheet.

3 Group Sheet 1, Sheet 2, Sheet 3, and Sheet 4. Continue with the following calculations and formatting:

- In cell C24, use the SUM function to calculate the total items ordered on each sheet.
- In cell D24, create a formula to calculate the number of total items shipped on each sheet.
- In cell D25, create a formula to calculate the Total NOT shipped. Subtract the amount ordered minus the amount shipped.
- In cell K13, create a formula to calculate totals. Multiply the number shipped by the Unit Price. Use the fill handle to copy the formula to cells K14:K22.

(Project 2C Dental Invoice continues on the next page)

Dental Assisting

GO! Make It | Project 2C Dental Invoice (continued)

- In cells I13:K13, apply Accounting format. In cells I14:K22, apply Comma Style.
- In cell K24, create a formula to calculate the subtotal.
- In cell K27, create a formula to calculate the local tax based on the rates in cell H27. In cell K28, create a formula to calculate the state tax based on the rate in cell H28.
- In cell K29, create a formula to calculate the Total. In cells I29:K29, change the font to 12 pt, bold, and then apply a Dark Blue, Text 2, Lighter 40% fill.

4 Ungroup the worksheets.

- In Sheet 2, cell K26, change the cell to Accounting format.
- Rename Sheet 1 **Jan 2012** rename Sheet 2 **Feb 2012** rename Sheet 3 **Mar 2012** rename Sheet 4 **Apr 2012** and then rename Sheet 5 **Summary** Add a color to each tab.
- Format the Summary sheet. Merge and Center cells A1:C1, change the font to Calibri 16 pt, and then apply bold. Merge and Center cells A2:C2, change the font to Calibri 12 pt, and then apply bold. Merge and Center cells A3:C3, change the font to Calibri 12 pt, and then apply bold. In cells A1:C3, apply a Dark Blue, Text 2, Lighter 60% fill.
- Size column A as 130 pixels. Size column B as 155 pixels. Size column C as 170 pixels.
- In cells A4:C4, apply a Dark Blue, Text 2, Darker 25% fill. Change the text to white, apply bold, and then center the cells.
- In cells B5:B8, create cell references for the Items Shipped for each month, and then center the cells.
- In cells C5:C8, create cell references for the Amount, using the Subtotals for each month.
- In cells, A5:C8, apply a Dark Blue, Text 2, Lighter 80% fill.
- Center the Summary horizontally on the page. Set the top margin to 2". In the center section of the header, insert the **e2C_Smile** picture. In the left section of the footer, insert the code for the file name. In the right section of the footer, insert the code for the date. Set the Print Area in Page Layout to ensure the table is horizontally centered.
- Create a 2-D Clustered Column chart showing the Amount for each month. Move the chart to a new Sheet named **Summary Chart** Use Chart Style 26. Above the chart, add the title **Smiling Families Dental Supply Expenses** on the first line of the title. On the second line of the title, add **January 2012 – April 2012** Change the font in the title to Calibri 20 pt. Add **Month** to the Horizontal Axis title, and then add **Amount** as Vertical Axis Horizontal Title. Change the font in the axis titles to Calibri 18 pt. Delete the legend.
- In the Summary Chart worksheet, at the top of the chart above the February column, insert a text box that says **Highest Month** Apply the Moderate Effect - Blue, Accent 1 shape style. Format the text in the text box to Calibri 16 pt bold, and then center the text in the box. Size the box .4" high and 1.6" wide. Draw a line arrow from the box to the January column showing that it had the highest amount. Add a color to the sheet tab. Move the Summary Chart worksheet so that it is after the Summary worksheet.

5 Check the worksheets for spelling and grammar errors and correct any errors you find.

Save the workbook and submit it as directed.

End **You have completed Project 2C**

Dental Assisting

Apply the skills from these Objectives:

1. Enter Data in a Worksheet
2. Construct and Copy Formulas and Use the SUM Function
3. Format Cells with Merge & Center and Cell Styles
4. Check Spelling in a Worksheet
5. Construct Formulas for Mathematical Operations
6. Format a Worksheet
7. Use IF Functions and Apply Conditional Formatting
8. Navigate a Workbook and Rename Worksheets
9. Edit and Format Multiple Worksheets at the Same Time
10. Create a Summary Sheet
11. Chart Data with a Pie Chart
12. Format a Pie Chart

GO! Think | Project **2D** Dental Order

Project Files

For Project 2D, you will need the following file:

    e2D_Dental_Order

You will save your workbook as:

    Lastname_Firstname_2D_Dental_Order

One of your duties at Smiling Families Dental Group is to keep track of dental supplies for the entire office and order them on a regular basis. You have created a workbook that contains a worksheet for each supplier, and you also maintain a summary worksheet that keeps track of the total inventory value on hand. You will modify your existing workbook by inserting formulas to calculate the value of current inventory, and then you will insert an IF function to alert you when you need to reorder a particular item. You will format the worksheets to make them easier to read and update.

Open the file **e2D_Dental_Order**, and then save it in the Dental Assisting Excel folder as **Lastname_Firstname_2D_Dental_Order**

1 Review the placement of the data on sheets 1 through 4. On sheet 3, move the contents of A18 to A19 to match the other worksheets. Group Sheet 1, Sheet 2, Sheet 3, and Sheet 4, and then modify the group as follows:

- Change the orientation to Landscape.
- Merge and center the cells in the title row, and then apply a fill color. Increase the font size, and then change the font color.
- In rows 3, 4, and 5, apply a fill color to the cells containing the supplier name, address, supplier number, and purchasing department information. Apply bold to the text in those three rows.
- In the left section of the header, insert the text **Supply Ordering and Tracking** In the right section of the header, insert a code for the current date; and then in the center section of the footer, insert a code for the file name.
- In row 8, center the column headings, bold the text, and then wrap the text. Apply a fill color to cells in the row. Autofit the row height. In cell F8, change the word Price to **Cost**.
- AutoFit all of the columns except A and L.
- In cells G9:G15, center the numbers.
- In cell H9, create a formula to calculate the inventory value using the unit cost and quantity in stock. Use the fill handle to copy this formula to cells H10:H15.
- In cell H19, sum the Inventory Value. Format the cell in Accounting format with bottom double border.
- In cell I9, insert an IF function to display the text ORDER when the Qty in Stock is less than 10. Copy the function to cells I10:I15. This will alert you to order more of each item when your current inventory falls below 10.
- Format the cells in the worksheet using Accounting format and Comma Style.

(Project 2D Dental Order continues on the next page)

Dental Assisting

GO! Think | Project **2D** Dental Order (continued)

2 Ungroup the sheets.

3 Rename the worksheet tabs with the names of the suppliers.

4 Simulate ordering supplies by inserting dates in the Order Date and Qty. Ordered columns for at least five items.

5 If necessary, adjust the margins and column widths so that each worksheet fits on one page.

6 On the Monthly Summary sheet, modify the following:

- Format the rows with similar fill color and fonts as the other worksheets but use Portrait orientation. Center the summary data on the worksheet horizontally.

- In cells B5:B8, insert cell references to the detail worksheets for Total Inventory Value for each supplier.

- In cell B10, insert a formula to sum the Total Inventory Value.

- In cell C5, insert a formula with absolute cell referencing to calculate the percentage that each supplier's inventory represents of the total inventory. Copy the formula to C6:C8 to display *% of Total Inventory* for each supplier. Format cells C5:C8 with Percent Style with one decimal place, and then center the figures.

- Create a pie chart that shows the percentage of total inventory for each supplier. Select a Chart Layout and Chart Style.

- Add and position a text box on the Monthly Summary sheet to call attention to one of the totals.

7 Check the worksheets for spelling and grammar errors and correct any errors you find. Save the workbook and submit it as directed.

End **You have completed Project 2D** —————————————————————————

Fire Science

Apply the skills from these Objectives:

1. Enter Data in a Worksheet
2. Construct and Copy Formulas and Use the SUM Function
3. Format Cells with Merge & Center and Cell Styles
4. Chart Data to Create a Column Chart
5. Check Spelling in a Worksheet
6. Construct Formulas for Mathematical Operations
7. Edit Values in a Worksheet
8. Format a Worksheet
9. Use the SUM, AVERAGE, MEDIAN, MIN and MAX Functions
10. Use COUNTIF and IF Functions and Apply Conditional Formatting
11. Navigate a Workbook and Rename Worksheets
12. Edit and Format Multiple Worksheets at the Same Time
13. Create a Summary Sheet

GO! Make It | Project 2E Chow Spreadsheet

Project Files

For Project 2E, you will need the following files:

e2E_Chow_Spreadsheet
e2E_CSFD_Logo

You will save your workbook as:

Lastname_Firstname_2E_Chow_Spreadsheet

Project Results

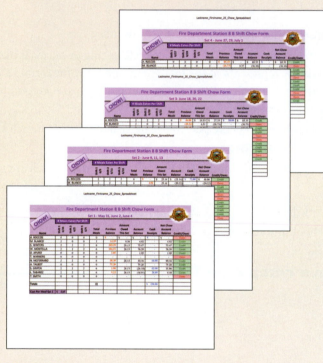

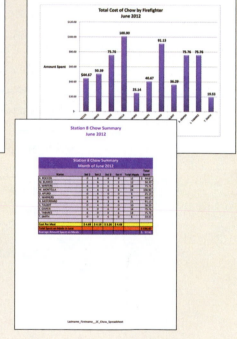

Figure 2.3
Project 2E Chow Spreadsheet

(Project 2E Chow Spreadsheet continues on the next page)

GO! Make It | Project 2E Chow Spreadsheet (continued)

You are the driver on B shift at Fire Station 8, and it's your responsibility to keep the Chow Spreadsheet for your group for the next month. You work three 24-hour shifts from 8 a.m. to 8 a.m. every other day for three days, and then you have four days off. Each day in a three-day set is referred to as a shift. Every shift will alternate cooks, and each cook is responsible for purchasing the food for the two meals they will prepare on the day they cook. Each cook turns in the receipts for the food they buy. As the shift progresses, it's important to keep track of how much each cook has spent, how much each meal cost, and how much each firefighter owes for the meals they eat. Those who haven't cooked may owe money until it is their time to cook. Each cook tries to keep the total cost for his meals under $10/day. This sheet is used by all the drivers who rotate this responsibility, so it needs to be accurate and up-to-date for each shift.

Create a new folder to store your Excel files, and then name the folder **Fire Science Excel**

From the student files that accompany this textbook, locate and open the file **e2E_Chow_Spreadsheet**, and then save the file in your Fire Science Excel folder as **Lastname_Firstname_2E_Chow_Spreadsheet** In the workbook, follow the steps to modify the worksheets shown in Figure 2.3.

1 Group Sheet 1, Sheet 2, Sheet 3, and Sheet 4, and then modify the group as follows:

- Change the orientation to Landscape.
- Change the top margin to 1", and center the data horizontally on the page.
- In cells A5:K19, apply All Borders.
- In the center section of the header, insert the code for the file name.
- Merge and center cells A1:K1. Format the text as Calibri 18 pt, apply bold, and then change the color to Purple in Standard colors. Apply a Purple, Accent 4, Lighter 60% fill. Size the row to 45 pixels.
- Merge and center cells A2:K2. Format the text as Calibri 14 pt, apply bold, and then change the color to Purple in Standard colors. Apply a Purple, Accent 4, Lighter 80% fill. Size the row to 40 pixels. Apply a bottom double border.
- Size row 3 to 30 pixels. In cells A3:K3, apply a Purple, Accent 4, Lighter 60% fill. Select cells B3:D3, merge and center them, and then add a thick box border. Bold the text, and then change it to 12 pt and white. Apply a Standard Purple fill.
- Size row 4 to 75 pixels. In cells E4:J4, wrap the text, center it, and then apply bold. Size columns E through J to 85 pixels. AutoFit column K, and then bold cell K4.
- In cells B4:D4, change the alignment to 90 degrees, and then bold and center the column headings vertically and horizontally within the cells. In columns B, C, and D, size the width to 70 pixels. In cells A4:K4, apply a Purple, Accent 4, Lighter 60% fill, and then add a bottom double border.
- In cell A4, center and bold the column heading. AutoFit column A.
- In cells F5:F15, format the text Standard Red and bold.
- In cells I5:I17, format the text Standard Blue and bold.
- In cells A19:B19, apply a Purple Accent, Lighter 40% fill and bold. Autofit Column A.

(Project 2E Chow Spreadsheet continues on the next page)

Fire Science

GO! Make It | Project 2E Chow Spreadsheet (continued)

2 Ungroup the worksheets.

- In the first worksheet, in cell A2, insert a WordArt using the WordArt Text Style Gradient Fill - Purple, Accent 4, Reflection. Change the text to 20 pt. Apply the Shape Style, Subtle Effect - Purple, Accent 4. Type the text **CHOW!** Size the WordArt to .4" by 1.06". Rotate the WordArt approximately 45 degrees, and then position it in the upper left corner of the worksheet in cells A2 and A3. Copy the WordArt to the Clipboard.

- In the first worksheet, insert the **e2E_CSFD_Logo** graphic in the upper right corner of the worksheet. Size the graphic 1" high by 1.19" wide. Apply the Soft Edge Oval picture effect. Copy the graphic to the Clipboard.

- In worksheet 2, in cell A2:A3, paste the WordArt from the Clipboard to worksheet 2 and position it between the A2 and A3 cell so that it is in the same location as worksheet 1. Paste the logo graphic in the upper right corner of worksheet 2. Using the skills you just practiced, paste the WordArt and logo graphic to worksheet 3 and worksheet 4.

- Rename Sheet 1 **Set 1** rename Sheet 2 **Set 2** rename Sheet 3 **Set 3** rename Sheet 4 **Set 4** and rename Sheet 5 **Chow Summary** Change the color of each tab to a color of your choice.

3 Group Sheet 1, Sheet 2, Sheet 3, and Sheet 4, and then continue with the following calculations:

- In cell E5, insert a formula that totals the meals for each name using SUM function. Use the fill handle to copy the formula to cells E6:E15. Center cells E5:E17.

- In cell I17, insert a formula to SUM total spent on food in Cook Receipts, and then apply Accounting format.

- In cell E17, insert a formula to SUM the total number of meals, and then apply bold and center.

- In cell B19, insert a formula to calculate the cost per meal by dividing Total Cook Receipts by Total Meals.

- In cell G5, insert a formula that will figure the amount owed by multiplying the number of meals for each firefighter by the cost per meal. Use absolute cell references for the cost per meal. Use the fill handle to copy the formula to cells G6:G15.

- In cell H5, insert a formula to calculate the account balance for each name by subtracting Amount Owed This Set from the Previous Balance. Use the fill handle to copy this formula to cells H6:H15.

- In cell J5, insert a formula to calculate the Net Chow Account Balance by adding Account Balance to Cook Receipts. Use the fill handle to copy this formula to cells J6:J15.

4 Ungroup the worksheets.

- In the Set 2 worksheet, in cell F5, insert a cell reference formula that uses the Net Chow Account Balance for each name from Set 1. Copy the formula to cells F6:F15. This copies all the Net Chow Account Balances from Set 1 to Set 2.

- In the Set 3 worksheet, in cell F5, insert a cell reference formula that uses the balance from Set 2. Copy the formula to cells F6:F15. This copies all the Net Chow Account Balances from Set 2 to Set 3.

- In the Set 4 worksheet, in cell F5, insert a cell reference formula that uses the balance from Set 3. Copy the formula to cells F6:F15. This copies all the Net Chow Account Balances from Set 3 to Set 4.

(Project 2E Chow Spreadsheet continues on the next page)

GO! Make It | Project 2E Chow Spreadsheet (continued)

5 Group Sheet 1, Sheet 2, Sheet 3, and Sheet 4, and then complete the following steps:

- In the Set 1 worksheet, in cell K5, insert the following formula **=IF(J5>0,"Credit","Owes")** This formula inserts the word *Credit* or *Owes* depending on the positive or negative balance. Use the fill handle to copy the formula to cells K6:K15. Center cells K5:K15.

- In cells F5:J5, apply Accounting format.

- In cells F6:J15, apply Comma Style.

6 Ungroup the worksheets, and then continue with the following steps:

- In the Set 1 worksheet, create Conditional Formatting that highlights cells that contain the text *Credit* in Green Fill with Dark Green Text. In cell K5, select Conditional Formatting Style, Highlight Cells Rules, and Text that Contains. Type **Credit** and then select Green Fill with Dark Green Text. Use the fill handle to copy the formatting to cells K6:K15 for each name. In cell K5, select Conditional Formatting Style, Highlight Cells Rules, and Text that Contains. Type **Owes** and then select Light Red Fill with Dark Red Text. Use the fill handle to copy the formatting to cells K6:K15. Use the Format Painter to copy the conditional formatting to the other three worksheets.

- In the Chow Summary worksheet, merge and center cells A1:G1. Merge and center cells A2:G2. In cells A1:A2, change the font to 16 pt, white, and bold. Apply a Standard Purple fill. Adjust the row height so the text fits if necessary.

- In cell G3, wrap the text. In cells A3:G3, center and bold the column headings. AutoFit all columns.

- In cells A3:G3, apply a Purple, Accent 4, Lighter 40% fill.

- In cells A16:G16, apply Standard Yellow fill and bold.

- In cells A17:G17, apply Standard Red fill and bold.

- In cells A18:G18, apply Standard Purple fill. Change the text to white and bold.

- In the center section of the header, on the first line, insert **Station 8 Chow Summary** On the second line, insert **June 2012** Change the font to 18 pt Standard Purple, and then apply bold.

- In the center section of the footer, insert a code for the file name.

- Change the top margin to 2″. Center the worksheet horizontally on the page.

- In cell B4, insert a cell reference for the total meals for Set 1 for A. Roccos. Use the fill handle to copy the formula to cells B5:B14.

- In cell C4, insert a cell reference for the total meals for Set 2 for A. Roccos. Use the fill handle to copy the formula to cells C5:C14. Complete the same steps for Set 3 and Set 4. Center cells B4:F14.

- In cell F4, insert a formula to SUM the total number of meals. Use the fill handle to copy the formula to cells F5:F14.

- In cells B16:E16, insert a formula and use cell references to insert the cost per meal for each set.

- In cell G4, insert a formula that calculates the total spent on meals for each firefighter. Multiply the number of meals in each set by the cost per meal in each set. You will use an absolute cell reference every time you multiply the cost per meal. Use the formula **=(B4*B16)+(C4*C16)+ (D4*D16)+(E4*E16)** Use the fill handle to copy the formula to cells G5:G14. AutoFit column G. In cell G4, apply Accounting format. For cells G5:G14, apply Comma Style.

(Project 2E Chow Spreadsheet continues on the next page)

GO! Make It | Project 2E Chow Spreadsheet (continued)

- In cell G17, insert a formula that calculates the total spent on meals in June.
- In cell G18, insert a formula that calculates the average amount spent on meals for the month of June. Use the AVG function for all the totals paid by each firefighter.
- In cells A4:G18, apply All Borders.
- In cells A4:G15, apply a Purple, Accent 4, Lighter 80% fill.
- Insert a 2-D Clustered column chart that shows each firefighter's name and the total amount spent. Move the chart to a new sheet, and then name the sheet **Chow Chart** Apply Chart Style 30. Add a title above the chart and insert **Total Cost of Chow by Firefighter** On the second line of the title, insert **June 2012** Change the font to 24 pt. Add the title **Firefighter** for the horizontal axis below the axis and add a horizontal title **Amount Spent** for the vertical axis. Change the font for the axis titles to 14 pt. Delete the legend. Show the data labels, and then change the font to 14 pt bold. Move the Chow Chart worksheet so it is positioned after the Chow Summary worksheet. Add a color to the Chow Chart worksheet tab.

7 Check all worksheets for spelling and grammar errors and correct any errors you find.

Save the workbook and submit it as directed.

End **You have completed Project 2E** ————————————————

Fire Science

GO! Think | Project 2F Station Staffing

Project Files

For Project 2F, you will need the following files:

> e2F_Station_Staffing
> e2F_CSFD_Logo

You will save your workbook as:

> Lastname_Firstname_2F_Station_Staffing

One of your duties at Fire Station 8 is to maintain staffing records for your shift. At Station 8, each shift works 24 hours per day in a set of three days. You have worked the first day of the three-day set and will now prepare your workbook to record the hours scheduled for the next two days of the set. You will copy an existing worksheet to use for these two days. The last sheet in the workbook lists the entire staff for Station 8. You will create formulas to calculate the pay per position for a set, total the years of service to the department, total the pay per set, and calculate the percentage of staffing expense for each person. You will format this worksheet as a table, and then create a pie chart that visually displays the percentage of staffing expense for each person.

Open the file **e2F_Station_Staffing**, and then save it to your Fire Science Excel folder as **Lastname_Firstname_2F_Station_Staffing**

1 Review the Set 2 - Shift 1 worksheet to familiarize yourself with the data in each column and the codes. Note that multiple rows are used when people have more than one assignment per day, such as Kevin Martinez.

2 You are going to copy the Set 2 - Shift 1 worksheet twice to use for the other two days of the set. Before you do that, make the following modifications:

- Change the orientation to Landscape.

- Merge the cells in each of the first four rows. For each row, apply bold to the text, apply a fill color of your choice, and then change the font type and size.

- In row 4, change the date format to Long Date to display the day and month spelled out.

- In the left section of the header, insert your name, insert the code for the date in the right section of the header, and then insert a code for the file name in the center section of the footer.

- Center the column headings, apply bold to them, and then wrap the text.

- Using the RANK column as a guide, apply fill color to rows using the same color for those with the same job position.

- If necessary, adjust the column widths so that the worksheet fits on one page, and then center, left, or right align the data in each column.

- Apply a border of your choice to the cells in rows 1, 2, 3, and 4 on the worksheet.

(Project 2F Station Staffing continues on the next page)

GO! Think | Project **2F** Station Staffing (continued)

3 Copy the worksheet two times for the remaining two days of the set. The two new worksheets should be inserted after the Set 2 - Shift 1 worksheet.

4 For the second worksheet, change the date in row 4 to June 11. For the third worksheet, change the date in row 4 to June 13.

5 On sheets June 11 and June 13, delete rows 12 and 16 because Kevin Martinez and Thomas Blankenship will not have multiple assignments as they did on June 9. Change the start time for their shifts to 8:00.

6 Rename the worksheets tabs **June 9** and **June 11** and **June 13** according to the date in row 4.

7 The worksheet named Station 8 Staffing lists the name of each firefighter, rank, years of service, hourly rate of pay, and hours per set. Review the data on this worksheet and then modify it as follows:

- In row 1, merge and center the data and apply shading to the cells.

- In cell D14, use the SUM function to display the total years of service for the combined staff. In cell F14, use the SUM function to display the total number of hours worked per set.

- In cell G3, insert a formula to calculate the pay per set for the individual firefighter. Copy the formula to cells G4:G12. In cell G14, use the SUM function to display the total pay per set.

- In cell H3, insert a formula with absolute cell referencing to calculate the percentage each individual's pay is of the total pay per set. Copy the formula to cells H4:H12.

- Format your worksheet by applying Accounting format and Comma Style to columns with dollar amounts and Percent Style to the column with percentages. Center the columns with rank, service years, and hours per set. Autofit the columns.

- Format A2:H14 cells of this worksheet as a table. Sort the table by years of service. Perform another sort by last name.

- Create a chart that displays each individual's percentage of the total pay per set. Move the chart to a new sheet, and then name the sheet **Staffing Chart**

- Insert the **e2F_CSFD_Logo** on one or more of the worksheets.

8 Check all worksheets for spelling and grammar errors and correct any errors you find. Save the workbook and submit it as directed.

End You have completed Project 2F ———————————————

Paralegal

GO! Make It | Project 2G Stockholder Ledger

Project Files

For Project 2G, you will need the following file:

    e2G_Stockholder_Ledger

You will save your workbook as:

    Lastname_Firstname_e2G_Stockholder_ Ledger

Project Results

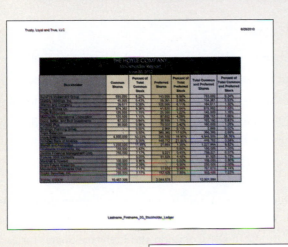

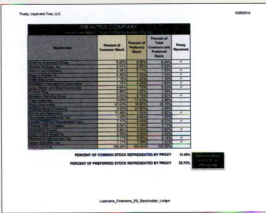

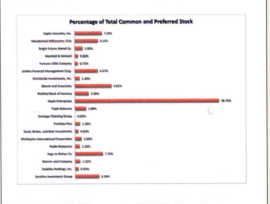

Figure 2.4

Project 2G Stockholder Ledger

(Project 2G Stockholder Ledger continues on the next page)

GO! Make It | Project **2G** Stockholder Ledger (continued)

Create a new folder to store your Excel files, and then name the folder **Paralegal Excel** From the student files that accompany this textbook, locate and open the file **e2G_Stockholder_Ledger**, and then save the file in your Paralegal Excel folder as **Lastname_Firstname_2G_Stockholder_Ledger**. Group the two worksheets, and then modify both simultaneously as follows:

1 In the left section of the header, insert the text **Trusty, Loyal, and True, LLC** In the right section of the header, insert the code for the current date, and then in the center section of the footer, insert the code for the file name.

2 Change the page orientation to Landscape.

3 Ungroup the sheets.

4 Modify Sheet 1 as follows:

- Change the top margin to 1.5", and then center the data horizontally on the sheet.

- In row 1, merge and center cells A1:G1, and then change the font to Century Gothic 16 pt.

- In row 2, merge and center cells A2:G2, and then change the font to Century Gothic 14 pt.

- In row 3, merge and center cells A3:G3; apply Date formatting to display month spelled out, day, and year as shown in Figure 2.4; and then change the font to Century Gothic 12 pt.

- In rows 1, 2, and 3, apply Fill Color Black, Text 1, change the font color to White, Background 1.

- Format row 4 by bolding the text, middle and center aligning the text, and applying wrap text. Autofit rows 1-4.

- In cell F5, insert a formula to add Common and Preferred Shares for each stockholder, and then copy the formula to the cells F6:F24. This is the Total Common and Preferred Shares for each stockholder.

- Apply Comma Style with no decimal places to nonadjacent columns Common Shares, Preferred Shares, and Total Common and Preferred Shares.

- In cells B25, D25, and F25, use the SUM function to total the Common Shares, Preferred Shares, and Total Common and Preferred Shares columns.

- In cell C5, insert a formula with absolute cell referencing to calculate the Percent of Common Stock for each stockholder based on the total in row 25. Use the fill handle to copy the formula to cells C6:C24.

- Using the skills you practiced, in cell E5, insert a formula with absolute cell referencing to calculate the Percent of Preferred Stock. In cell G5, insert a formula with absolute cell referencing to calculate the Percent of Total Common and Preferred Stock. Use the fill handle to copy the formulas to E6:E24 and G6:G24.

- In columns C, E, and G, format the numbers in Percent Style with two decimal places, and then center align the percentages.

- In cells A4:A25, apply Fill Color Black, Text 1, Lighter 50%; in cells B4:C25, apply Fill Color Tan, Background 2, Darker 10%; in cells D4:E25, apply Fill Color Tan, Background 2, Darker 25%; and then in cells F4:G25, apply Fill Color White, Background 1, Darker 25%.

- In cells A4:G24, apply All Borders and then apply a Thick Bottom Border to cells A25:G25.

- Rename Sheet 1 **Stockholder Report**

(Project 2G Stockholder Ledger continues on the next page)

GO! Make It | Project **2G** Stockholder Ledger (continued)

5 Modify Sheet 2 as follows:

- Change the top and bottom margins to .8", and then center the data horizontally on the sheet.

- In row 1, merge and center cells A1:E1; change the font to Century Gothic 16 pt; apply Fill Color Black, Text 1; and then change the font color to White, Background 1.

- In row 2, merge and center cells A2:E2; change the font to Century Gothic 12 pt; apply Fill Color Black, Text 1; and then change the font color to White, Background 1.

- Format row 3 by bolding the text, middle and center aligning the text, and applying wrap text. Autofit row 3.

- In cell B4, the Percent of Common Stock column, insert a cell reference to the Stockholder Report worksheet. Copy the cell reference to cells B5:B23. Follow the same procedure to insert cell references for Percent of Preferred Stock and Percent of Total Common and Preferred Stock.

- In cells B24:D24, sum the percentages in each column to verify a total of 100%.

- Insert a check mark symbol, Wingdings character 252, in the Proxy Received column for cells E4, E6, E7, E8, E9, E10, E12, E16, E18, E20, E22, and E23. Center the symbols in the column.

- Autofit rows 4 through 24.

- In cell E26, insert a formula to display the Percent of Common Stock Represented by Proxy. Hint: Use the point and click method to add the percentages in column B for the companies marked with a check mark. In cell E28, insert a formula to display the Percent of Preferred Stock Represented by Proxy. Hint: Use the point and click method to add the percentages in column C for the companies marked with a check mark. Bold the text in rows 26 and 28.

- In cells A3:A24, apply Fill Color Black, Text 1, Lighter 50%; in cells B3:B24, apply Fill Color Tan, Background 2, Darker 10%; in cells C3:C24, apply Fill Color Tan, Background 2, Darker 25%; in cells D3:D24, apply Fill Color White, Background 1, Darker 25%; and then in cells E3:E24, apply Fill Color White, Background 1, Darker 5%.

- Apply All Borders to cells A3 to E24.

- Rename Sheet 2 **Proxy Tabulation**

- Insert a text box with the text **Need two thirds or 66% for an official vote** and then position it to the right of cell E26. Center the text as shown in Figure 2.4. Size the text box .7" high by 1.3" wide. Apply Shape Style Light 1 Outline, Fill Color Black, Dark 1 to the text box.

6 Create a chart as follows:

- On the Stockholder Report worksheet, insert a Clustered Bar chart with the data in cells A5:A24 and G5:G24.

- Move the chart to a new sheet named **Ownership Chart**

- Format the chart by applying Chart Layout 2 and Chart Style 28.

- Replace Chart Title with **Percentage of Total Common and Preferred Stock**

- Change the layout of the legend to None.

- Move the Ownership Chart worksheet to the right of Proxy Tabulation.

7 Check all worksheets for spelling and grammar errors and correct any errors you find. Save the workbook and submit it as directed.

End **You have completed Project 2G** _____

Paralegal

GO! Think | Project 2H Billable Hours

Project Files

For Project 2H, you will need the following file:

    e2H_Billable_Hours

You will save your workbook as:

    Lastname_Firstname_2H_Billable_Hours

One of your new duties at the law firm of Trusty, Loyal, and True, LLC is to maintain a record of billable hours for specific cases. You have been provided with a workbook that contains a rough design along with the estimated billable hours for a case.

Open the file **e2H_Billable_Hours**, and then save it to your Paralegal Excel folder as **Lastname_Firstname_2H_Billable_Hours** Modify the existing worksheet as follows:

1 Change the orientation to Landscape.

2 Merge and center the cells in each of the first four rows across columns A through G, format the text in bold, and then apply fill color. For each row, change the font type, size, and color.

3 In the center section of the footer, insert a code for the file name.

4 In rows 5 and 7, center the text, apply bold, and then wrap the text.

5 In cell A6, insert the text **Hourly Rate** and then right align the text.

6 In cells B6, C6, and D6, insert hourly rates for each person as follows. For Karen Garcia, insert **$300** for Rob Li, insert **$200** and for Karla Hoyle, insert **$80** The content of these cells will be used in another formula to calculate the total actual hourly fees.

7 In cells B19, C19, and D19, sum the total estimated billable hours for each person.

8 In cell B21, create a formula to calculate the total estimated hourly fees for Karen Garcia based on the hourly rate and total billable hours. Insert a similar formula in cells C21 and D21.

9 To the right of column B, insert a column to record the actual hours of work by Karen. Insert a column to the right of column D to record actual hours for Rob Li. In cells C7, E7, and G7, type a column name **Actual Hours** The data for the Actual Hours columns will be inserted in a later step.

10 Although there are no actual hours in the worksheet yet, you will create formulas to sum the actual hours and calculate actual hourly fees. In row 19, create a formula to sum the total actual hours. In cell C22, create a formula to calculate the total actual hourly fees for Karen Garcia. Copy the formula to cells E22 and G22 to calculate fees for Li and Hoyle.

(Project 2H Billable Hours continues on the next page)

Paralegal

GO! Think | Project 2H Billable Hours (continued)

11 Apply a fill color of your choice to columns containing data for Karen Garcia. Apply a different fill color to columns containing data for Rob Li and a different fill color to columns containing data for Karla Hoyle. Apply borders to each shaded group of cells to clearly separate the data for each of the three people working on the case.

12 Apply Accounting format and/or Comma Style based on the data in the cells. Center align the Hours columns.

13 If necessary, adjust the margins and/or column widths so that the worksheet fits on one page.

Create a pie chart to show the percentage of the total estimated hourly fees earned by each person. Move the chart to a new worksheet, and then name it **Estimated Fees Chart**

Create and copy new worksheets as follows:

1 Create a new worksheet to track the actual hours that Karla Hoyle, the paralegal, works on each task. Name the sheet **Paralegal Actual Hours** Copy the tasks from Firm Billable Hours worksheet to a column in this worksheet including the column heading Description.

2 In the two columns to the right of *Description*, type column headings **Date** and **# of Hours** These columns will be used to record actual dates and hours worked on each task. Insert hypothetical dates and numbers in these columns.

3 Total the hypothetical actual number of hours worked on each task. If necessary, insert additional rows or columns to record additional hypothetical dates and hours worked.

4 On the Firm Billable Hours worksheet, create a cell reference to display the result in the Actual Hours column on the Firm Billable Hours worksheet.

5 Insert a text box calling attention to the difference between estimated hours and actual hours for one of the tasks on either worksheet.

6 Copy this worksheet twice to create worksheets for future recording of actual dates and hours for the partner and the associate. Name the worksheets **Partner Actual Hours** and **Associate Actual Hours**. Delete the paralegal hours on the Partner and Associate worksheets.

7 Group the worksheets and apply Accounting format and/or Comma Style based on the data in the cells. Center the Hours columns.

8 Check all worksheets for spelling and grammar errors. Save the workbook and submit it as directed.

End You have completed Project 2H ⎯⎯⎯⎯⎯⎯⎯⎯⎯⎯

Excel | Chapter 2

Discipline-Specific Assignments

You will complete the following discipline-specific projects:

CULINARY ARTS

GO! Make It | Project 3A Culinary Recipe Database (p. 61)
GO! Think | Project 3B Culinary Arts Kitchen Inventory Database (p. 64)

DENTAL ASSISTING

GO! Make It | Project 3C Dental Inventory Database (p. 66)
GO! Think | Project 3D Dental Services Database (p. 70)

FIRE SCIENCE

GO! Make It | Project 3E Firefighter Certification Database (p. 72)
GO! Think | Project 3F Fire Science Inspections Database (p. 75)

PARALEGAL

GO! Make It | Project 3G Paralegal Caseload Database (p. 77)
GO! Think | Project 3H Legal Stockholders Database (p. 81)

Culinary Arts

GO! Make It | Project 3A Culinary Recipe Database

Project Files

For Project 3A, you will need the following files:

a3A_Recipe_Database (Access file)
a3A_Recipe_Ingredients (Excel table)

You will save your database as:

Lastname_Firstname_3A_Recipe_Database

Project Results

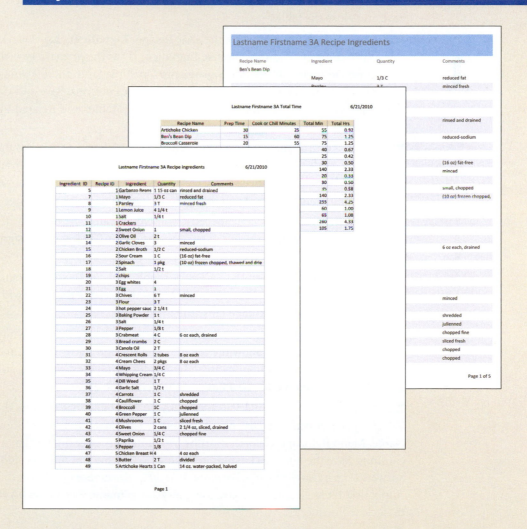

Figure 3.1
Project 3A Culinary Recipe Database

(Project 3A Culinary Recipe Database continues on the next page)

Access | Chapter 3

Culinary Arts

GO! Make It | Project **3A** Culinary Recipe Database (continued)

In this database project, you will open an existing recipe database. You will edit fields, import data from Excel to create a second table, create a relationship between the two tables, create and run queries, create a form, and create a report.

1 Create a new folder to store your Access files in and name the folder **Culinary Arts Access** From the student files that accompany this textbook, open **a3A_Recipe_Database**, and then save it to your Culinary Arts Access folder as **Lastname_Firstname_3A_Recipe_Database** Enable the content, open the **3A Recipes** table, and then become familiar with the data in the table.

2 In the 3A Recipes table, rename the Minutes Prep Time field **Prep Time** Move the Prep Time field to the left of the Cook or Chill Minutes field. Apply Best Fit to all of the columns. Save and close the table.

3 Create a table by importing the **a3A_Recipe_Ingredients** Excel workbook, use the first row as the column headings, and use Ingredient ID as the primary key. Name the table **Lastname Firstname 3A Recipe Ingredients** Open the table and become familiar with the information in the table. Apply Best Fit to all of the columns. Save and close the table. Ensure that objects on the Navigation Pane are grouped by Tables and Related Views. Be sure that all object names display fully.

4 Create a one-to-many relationship between the 3A Recipes table and the Lastname Firstname 3A Recipe Ingredients table using the Recipe ID field. Do not enforce referential integrity. Adjust the tables so that all fields are visible. Create a relationship report, and then save the report with the default name. Close the report and the Relationships pane.

5 Open the 3A Recipes table. Because you have created the relationship, you will see a plus sign or expand symbol to the left of each recipe name. Click the plus sign and you will see the ingredients listed for each recipe. Close the table.

6 Create a form based on the 3A Recipes table that can be used to enter more recipes. Use the Form Wizard, and then accept the default settings. Save the form with the name **Lastname Firstname 3A Recipes** and then close the form.

7 Create a query using the 3A Recipes table that answers the following question: *Which recipes are low fat recipes?* Show the Recipe Name, Menu Item, Source, and Low Fat fields in that order. Sort by Menu Item in ascending order. Apply Best Fit to all columns. Save the query as **Lastname Firstname 3A Low Fat** and then close the query.

8 Create a compound query using the 3A Recipes table that answers the following question: *Which Appetizer and Side Dish menu items have less than 150 calories?* Show the fields Recipe Name, Menu Item, and Calories. Sort by Menu Item in ascending order. Apply Best Fit to all columns. Save the query as **Lastname Firstname 3A Low Cal App and Side** Revise the query to answer: *Which Dessert items have more than 300 calories?* Sort in descending order by Calories. Apply Best Fit to all columns. Save the query as **Lastname Firstname 3A High Cal Desserts** and then close the query.

9 Create a calculated field query using the 3A Recipes table that answers the question: *What is the total time it takes to prepare a recipe including the prep time and cook or chill minutes?* Include the Recipe Name, Menu Item, Prep Time, and Cook or Chill Minutes. Delete the Menu Item field. Create a calculated field **Total Min** that calculates the Prep Time plus the Cook or Chill Minutes. Then create another calculated field **Total Hrs** that divides the Total Min by 60. Change the number format to Standard. Sort by Recipe Name in ascending order. Apply Best Fit to all the columns. Save the query as **Lastname Firstname 3A Total Time** Close the query.

(Project 3A Culinary Recipe Database continues on the next page)

GO! Make It | Project **3A** Culinary Recipe Database (continued)

10 Create a query using the 3A Recipes table that answers the question: *Which recipes serve 4 or more?* Show the Recipe Name, Source, Menu Item, and Servings. Sort by Menu item in ascending order. Save the query as **Lastname Firstname 3A Serves 4+** Close the query.

11 Create a query using the 3A Recipes table and the MAX function to show the highest Fat Grams, highest Mg Sodium, and highest Fiber Grams in any recipe. Apply Best Fit to all columns. Save the query as **Lastname Firstname 3A Max Fat Sod Fiber** Close the query.

12 Create a query using both tables and the COUNT function that shows the number of ingredients in each recipe. Show the Recipe Name and Ingredient. Sort in ascending order by Ingredient. Apply Best Fit to the columns. Save the query as **Lastname Firstname 3A # of Ingred** Close the query.

13 Create a query using both tables that answers the following question: *What are the ingredients in Recipe 2 and how much of each ingredient is needed?* Include the Recipe ID, Recipe Name, Ingredient, and Quantity fields. Sort in ascending order by Ingredient. Apply Best Fit to all columns. Save the query as **Lastname Firstname 3A Recipe 2 Ingred** Close the query.

14 Create a report using data from 3A Recipes and Lastname Firstname 3A Recipe Ingredients. Use the Report Wizard and add the Recipe Name, Ingredient, Quantity, and Comments to the report fields. View data by Recipe Name. Do not group or sort the data. Accept the Stepped Layout and Portrait Orientation and default settings. Save the report, and then name it **Lastname Firstname 3A Recipe Ingredients** Close the report.

15 Close the database and submit it as directed.

End **You have completed Project 3A** ——————————————

Access | Chapter 3

Culinary Arts

Apply the skills from
these objectives:

1 Create a Table
and Define Fields
in a New Blank
Database

2 Change the
Structure of Tables
and Add a Second
Table

3 Create and Use a
Form to Add and
Delete Records

4 Create Table
Relationships

5 Create a Query in
Design View

6 Sort Query Results

7 Specify Criteria in
a Query

8 Specify Numeric
Criteria in a Query

9 Use Compound
Criteria

10 Use Calculated
Fields in a Query

11 Calculate Statistics
and Group Data in
a Query

12 Create Reports by
Using the Blank
Report Tool or the
Report Wizard

13 Modify the Design
of a Report

14 Save and Close
a Database

GO! Think | Project 3B Culinary Arts Kitchen Inventory Database

Project Files

For Project 3B, you will need the following files:

New blank Access database
a3B_Cooking_Equipment (Excel file)

You will save your database as:

Lastname_Firstname_3B_Kitchen_Inventory

You are starting a catering business and have purchased some basic kitchen cookware, utensils, and cutlery. A local chef has advised you to keep records of your equipment and supplies. You will create a new database to store and track your inventory of equipment. You intend to maintain a list of restaurant suppliers from whom you will purchase your equipment and supplies. You will create a new blank database, create a table, create a form, import data from Excel to create a second table, create a relationship between the two tables, run queries, and create a report.

1 Create a new blank database and save it to your Culinary Arts Access folder. Name the database **Lastname_Firstname_3B_Kitchen_Inventory**

2 Create a new table to store data for three restaurant suppliers. Rename the ID field **Supplier ID** and then change the data type to text. Create names and select a data type for each field in your table based on the type of information listed below. SUP101, SUP102, and SUP103 are Supplier IDs. The first row of the table contains the Supplier ID. Save the table and name it **Lastname Firstname 3B Restaurant Suppliers** Type the following data in your table:

SUP101	SUP102	SUP103
King of Culinary Supplies	Baker's Dream	Wholesale Kitchen Equipment
5432 North Nevada Avenue	90 Frontage Road	6789 Pinion Bluffs Parkway
Colorado Springs	Denver	Colorado Springs
CO	CO	CO
80903	80266	80920
719-555-3211	303-555-4567	719-555-4958
www.kingofculinary.com	www.bakersdream.com	www.kitchenequip.com

3 Create a form for your table and save it with the default name.

4 Search the Internet to find three additional suppliers that sell cooking equipment. At each Web site, locate information about each supplier and then type the information for each of the three suppliers using the form.

5 Create a new table by importing the Excel workbook **a3B_Cooking_Equipment** into your database. Use the first row as column headings, and let Access add the primary key field. Name the table **Lastname Firstname 3B Cooking Equipment**

6 Open both tables. Look at the fields and the type of data that is in each table. Be sure the data type is set to Currency for fields with dollar amounts. Size all the columns in each table to Best Fit.

7 Create a relationship between the two tables using a field that is common to both tables. Enforce referential integrity. Save the relationship.

(Project 3B Culinary Arts Kitchen Inventory Database continues on the next page)

GO! Think | Project **3B** Culinary Arts Kitchen Inventory Database (continued)

8 Create a relationship report and save it with the default name.

9 Close the report and any open objects.

10 Create queries to answer the following questions and include fields of your choice. Input criteria and sort in Design View, and then run the queries. Save and name each query using words that are descriptive of the query results.

- Select a city, and then display only the suppliers that are in that city. What is the street address for each supplier in that city? Display the records in alphabetical order by supplier name.

- What baking pans are in your existing inventory, and what is the description of each pan?

- For which items do you have more than eight in your inventory?

- Based on the quantity in stock and the unit price, what is the value of each item? Format this value to display in Currency format. Sort by this new item value field in descending order.

- What are the sizes and quantities on hand for the items in the cutlery and utensils categories?

- Which items are missing a price? Use Is Null for the criteria. Search the Internet to find prices for those items, and then input the prices into the table.

- Based on the query that calculates item value, what is the total value or sum of your equipment in each category?

11 Create a report that displays your Cooking Equipment inventory. Group and sort the records as you desire. Modify the column width and change the orientation so that all data is visible. Name and save the report. Close the report and any open objects.

12 Close the database and submit it as directed.

 You have completed Project 3B

Dental Assisting

Apply the skills from these objectives:

1 Create a Table and Define Fields in a New Blank Database

2 Change the Structure of Tables and Add a Second Table

3 Create and Use a Form to Add and Delete Records

4 Create Table Relationships

5 Create a Query in Design View

6 Sort Query Results

7 Specify Criteria in a Query

8 Specify Numeric Criteria in a Query

9 Use Compound Criteria

10 Use Calculated Fields in a Query

11 Calculate Statistics and Group Data in a Query

12 Create a New Query from an Existing Query

13 Create Reports by Using the Blank Report Tool or the Report Wizard

14 Modify the Design of a Report

15 Save and Close a Database

GO! Make It | Project 3C Dental Inventory Database

Project Files

For Project 3C, you will need the following files:

New blank Access database
a3C_Dental_Inventory (Excel file)

You will save your database as:

Lastname_Firstname_3C_Dental_Inventory

Project Results

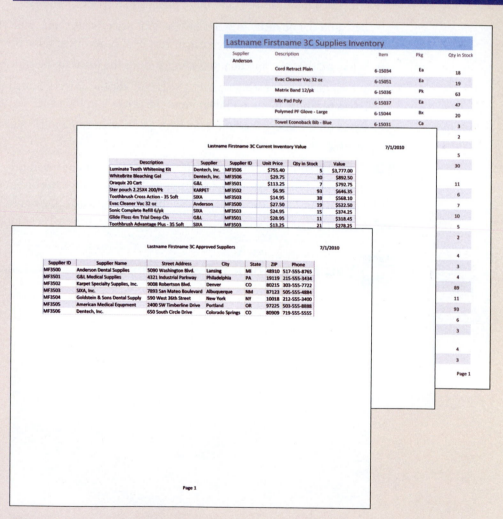

Figure 3.2
Project 3C Dental Inventory Database

(Project 3C Dental Inventory Database continues on the next page)

GO! Make It | Project **3C** Dental Inventory Database (continued)

In this database project, you will create a new database that tracks suppliers and inventory data. You will create a table, import data from Excel to create a second table, create a relationship between the two tables, run queries, create forms, add data, and create a report.

1 Create a new folder to store your Access files in, and then name the folder **Dental Assisting Access**

2 Create a new blank database, and then save it to your **Dental Assisting Access** folder. Name the database **Lastname_Firstname_3C_Dental_Inventory**

3 Create a suppliers table with the following fields, and then name it **Lastname Firstname 3C Approved Suppliers**

Field Name	Data type	Description
ID	AutoNumber	Assigned by Financial Services
Supplier Name	Text	
Street Address	Text	
City	Text	
State	Text	Enter the two-letter abbreviation
ZIP	Text	
Phone	Text	
Balance Due	Currency	

4 Change the ID field to Supplier ID field and data type to Text.

5 Change the properties for the State field to have a field size of 2 and then change the properties for the Balance Due field to two decimal places.

6 Create a form for this table, and then accept the default name. Switch to Form view, and then use the form to type the following data for seven suppliers and then close the table.

MF3500 Anderson Dental Supplies 5090 Washington Blvd. Lansing MI 48910 517-555-8765 493.70	MF3501 G&L Medical Supplies 4321 Industrial Parkway Philadelphia PA 19119 215-555-3434 1256.00	MF3502 Karpet Specialty Supplies, Inc. 9008 Robertson Blvd. Denver CO 80215 303-555-7722 836.41
MF3503 SIXA, Inc. 7893 San Mateo Boulevard Albuquerque NM 87123 505-555-4884 52.11	MF3504 Goldstein & Sons Dental Supply 590 West 36th Street New York NY 10018 212-555-3400 0.00	MF3505 American Medical Equipment 2400 SW Timberline Drive Portland OR 97225 503-555-8888 0.00
MF3506 Dentech, Inc. 650 South Circle Drive Colorado Springs CO 80909 719-555-5555 0.00		

(Project 3C Dental Inventory Database continues on the next page)

Access | Chapter 3

GO! Make It | Project 3C Dental Inventory Database (continued)

7 Import **a3C_Dental_Inventory** into the database as a new table. Use the first row as column headings, and let Access add the primary key field. Name the table **Lastname Firstname 3C Supplies Inventory** Modify the table as follows:

- Change the primary key field to Item, and then delete the ID field.
- Change the data type for the Unit Price field to Currency, and then set the field properties to two decimal places.
- Type a description for the Supplier ID field: **Enter six-digit MF number**
- Type a description for the Mfr field: **Enter manufacturer product code**
- Save the changes to the table.
- Create a form for this table and accept the default name.
- Switch to Form view, use the form to type two new items shown below, and then close the form.

19673	19824
Luminate Teeth Whitening Kit	WhiteBrite Bleaching Gel
Dz	Pk
Dentech, Inc.	Dentech, Inc.
MF3506	MF3506
400227	400361
$755.40	$29.75
5	30

- Open both tables. Look at the fields and note any fields that are common to both tables. Size all the columns in each table to Best Fit. Save and close the tables.
- Create a one-to-many relationship between the two tables using the Supplier ID field. Enforce referential integrity. Save the relationship.
- Create a relationship report, and then save it with the default name.
- Close the report and any open objects.

8 Based on the Lastname Firstname 3C Approved Suppliers table, create a query that shows all of the fields from the table, and then name the query **Lastname Firstname 3C Colorado Suppliers** Set the criteria to display only suppliers in Colorado. Run, save, and close the query.

9 Create the following queries based on the Lastname Firstname 3C Supplies Inventory table:

- Create a query that shows Item, Description, Pkg, Unit Price, and Qty in Stock. Sort by Qty in Stock in ascending order. Run the query, and then save it as **Lastname Firstname 3C Quantities in Stock** Close the query.
- Create a query that shows Item, Description, Pkg, Supplier, Unit Price, and Qty in Stock. Set the criteria to display only items with unit prices that are over $20. Sort by Unit Price in descending order. Run the query, and then save it as **Lastname Firstname 3C Inventory Items Over $20.** Close the query.
- Create a query that shows Supplier, Item, Description, Pkg, Unit Price, and Qty in Stock. Set the criteria to display only items supplied by Anderson and with Qty in Stock below 25. Run the query, and then save it as **Lastname Firstname 3C Anderson Qty Below 25** Close the query.

(Project 3C Dental Inventory Database continues on the next page)

GO! Make It | Project **3C** Dental Inventory Database (continued)

- Create a query to calculate the current value of the inventory in stock. Show Description, Supplier, Supplier ID, Unit Price, and Qty in Stock. Create a calculated field named Value that will multiply the unit price by the quantity in stock for each item. Sort by Value in descending order. Set the properties for the Value field to Currency with two decimals. Run the query, and then save it as **Lastname Firstname 3C Current Inventory Value** Close the query.

- Create a new query based on the Lastname Firstname 3C Current Inventory Value query that will total the Value for each supplier. Display only the Supplier name and Value fields and then sum the values. Set the properties for the SumofValue field to Currency with two decimals. Run the query, and then save it as **Lastname Firstname 3C Total Inventory Per Supplier** Close the query.

- Create a new query based on the Lastname Firstname 3C Current Inventory Value query. Show Description, Supplier, Qty in Stock, and Value. Set the criteria to display only those items supplied by SIXA. Clear the Show check box for the Supplier field. Run the query, and then save it as **Lastname Firstname 3C SIXA Current Inventory Value** Move the Qty in Stock column to the right of the Value field. Save and close the query.

 Using the Report Wizard, create a report based on the Lastname Firstname 3C Supplies Inventory table. Include Item, Description, Supplier, Pkg, and Qty in Stock fields and group by Supplier. Sort by description in ascending order and accept the Stepped and Portrait default settings. Finish creating the report, and then modify the report in Layout view. Modify column widths or reposition so that all data is visible. At the bottom of the page, ensure that the page number is positioned below the Qty in Stock column. Save the report, and then name it **Lastname Firstname 3C Supplies Inventory Report**.

11 Close all open objects. Close the database and submit it as directed.

End **You have completed Project 3C**

Access | Chapter 3

Dental Assisting

GO! Think | Project 3D Dental Services Database

Project Files

For Project 3D, you will need the following files:

a3D_Dental_Services (Excel File)
a3D_Dental_Services (Access file)

You will save your database as:

Lastname_Firstname_3D_Dental_Services

In this database project, you will work with a database for a dental office that includes a table with dental services and a table with patient information. You will open and edit a table, import data from Excel, create a relationship report, create and run queries, create a form, add data, and create a report.

1 From the student files that accompany this textbook, open the file **a3D_Dental_Services**, and then save it to your Dental Assisting Access folder as **Lastname_Firstname_3D_Dental_Services** Enable the content, and then open the **3D Patients** table. Become familiar with the information in the table. Apply Best Fit to all of the columns. Save and close the table.

2 Open the **3D Patient Billing** table. Move the Service Code field to the left of the Amt Billed field. Move the Next Appt field to the right of the Ins Paid field. Format the properties for dollar amounts to Currency. Apply Best Fit to all of the columns. Save and close the table. Ensure that objects on the Navigation Pane are grouped by Tables and Related Views. Be sure that all object names display fully.

3 Create a table by importing the **a3D_Dental_Services** Excel workbook. Use the first row as column headings and Service Code as the primary key. Save the table as **Lastname Firstname 3D Dental Services** Open the table. If you have a blank record at the beginning, delete it. Format the fields that are dollar amounts to Currency. Apply Best Fit to all columns. Save and close the table.

4 Create relationships showing all three tables in this order. First, create a one-to-one relationship between the 3D Patients and 3D Patient Billing tables using the Patient ID field. Enforce referential integrity. Then create a one-to-many relationship between the 3D Patient Billing Table and the Lastname Firstname 3D Dental Services table. Use the Service Code field to create the relationship. Enforce referential integrity. Create a relationship report. Save the report with the default name, and then close the report and any open objects.

5 Create a form using the Form Wizard for the 3D Patients table. Save the form as **Lastname Firstname 3D Patients** and then close the form.

6 Create a query that answers the question: *Which patients have had the procedure service code 00150?* Include the Last Name, First Name, and Service Code fields, and then sort by Last Name in ascending order. Save and close the query.

7 Create a query that answers the question: *What are the Diagnostic Services that cost $35 or more?* Sort by Fee in ascending order. Save the query. Revise the query to answer the question: *What are all the Restorative and Restorative Major services that cost more than $100?* Sort in ascending order by Service Type and in ascending order by Fee. Save and close the query.

8 Create a query that answers the question: *When are the next appointments for each patient?* Include the Last Name field and the First Name field along with the Next Appt field. Sort by Next Appt in ascending order. Save and close the query.

(Project 3D Dental Services Database continues on the next page)

GO! Think | Project **3D** Dental Services Database (continued)

9 Create a query with a calculated field that answers the question: *How much will each patient owe after the insurance payment?* Include Patient ID, Service Code, Amt Billed, and Ins Paid in that order. Create a calculated field **Acct Balance** that subtracts the Ins Paid from the Amt Billed. Be sure the fields with dollar amounts are formatted with Currency. Sort by Acct Balance in ascending order. Save and close the query.

10 Using the Acct Balance query and the SUM function to create a query showing the totals for the Amt Billed, Ins Paid, and Acct Balance. Save and close the query.

11 Using the Acct Balance query and the MAX Function, create a query showing the highest insurance payment. Save and close the query.

12 Create a report based on the Acct Balance query showing what patients owe. Use the Report Wizard and include all the fields. Do not group and Sort by Patient ID in Descending order. Modify the report in Layout view and ensure the fields fit horizontally on the page and are spaced evenly across the page. Center the data in the Service Code field. Save and close the report.

13 Close the database and submit it as directed.

 End **You have completed Project 3D** ————————————

Fire Science

GO! Make It | Project 3E Firefighter Certification Database

Project Files

For Project 3E, you will need the following files:

a3E_Fire_Certifications
a3E_Station8_Staff (Excel file)

You will save your database as:

Lastname_Firstname_3E_Fire_Certifications

Project Results

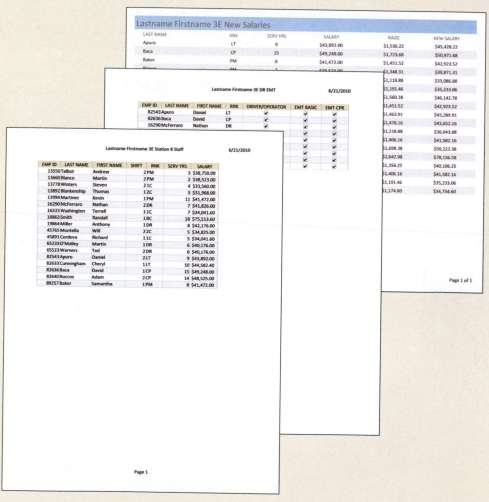

Figure 3.3

Project 3E Firefighter Certification Database

(Project 3E Firefighter Certification Database continues on the next page)

Fire Science

GO! Make It | Project 3E Firefighter Certification Database (continued)

In this database project, you will assist the fire chief in answering questions about the certifications that Fire Station 8 staff currently have. You will edit a table, import data from Excel to create a second table, create a relationship between the tables, run queries, create a form, and create a report.

1 Create a new folder to store your Access files in, and then name the folder **Fire Science Access**

2 From the student files that accompany this textbook, open **a3E_Fire_Certifications**, and then save it to your Fire Science Access folder as **Lastname_Firstname_3E_Fire_Certifications** Enable the content. Open the **3E Station 8 Certifications** table and become familiar with its contents.

3 In the 3E Station 8 Certifications table, rename the EMT 1 field name as **EMT BASIC** Rename the EMT 2 field name as **EMT CPR** Apply Best Fit to all columns. Save and close the table.

4 Create a table by importing the **a3E_Station8_Staff** Excel workbook. Use the first row as column headings, and use the EMP ID field as the primary key. Name the table **Lastname Firstname 3E Station 8 Staff** Open the table. Move the SHIFT field to the left of the RNK field. Apply Best Fit to all columns. Switch to Design view, and then add a Description for the SERV YRS that says **Total Years with Department** Change the properties for the RNK field to have a field size of 2. Save the table. When a message displays, *Some data will be lost*, click Yes. Close the table. Ensure that objects on the Navigation Pane are grouped by Tables and Related Views. Be sure that all object names display fully.

5 Create a form for the Lastname Firstname 3E Station 8 Staff table using the Form Wizard. Accept the default settings. Save it as **Lastname Firstname 3E Station 8 Staff** Close the form.

6 Create a one-to-one relationship between the two tables using the EMP ID field. Enforce referential integrity. Size the tables so all fields are visible. Create a relationship report, and then save it with the default name. Close the report and relationship.

7 Open the **Lastname Firstname 3E Station 8 Staff** table. You will see a plus sign or expand symbol to the left of the first field. When you click on the plus sign, you will see the certifications from the 3E Station 8 Certifications table for that firefighter. Open the **3E Station 8 Certifications** table. You will see the plus sign or expand symbol to the left of the first field. When you click on the plus sign, you will see the data for each firefighter.

8 Close all open objects.

9 Create a query that shows the EMP ID, LAST NAME, FIRST NAME, RNK, SERV YRS, and SHIFT. Sort by RNK in ascending order and by SERV YRS in ascending order. Apply Best Fit to all columns. Save the query as **Lastname Firstname 3E Staff RNK YRS SHIFT**

10 Revise the query to answer the following question: *Which firefighters work Shift 1?* Sort by LAST NAME in ascending order. Delete the SERV YRS field. Save the query as **Lastname Firstname 3E Shift 1** and then close the query.

11 Create a query to answer the question: *Which firefighters have 7 or more years of service?* Show LAST NAME, FIRST NAME, RNK, SERV YRS, and SALARY. Sort by RNK in ascending order and SERV YRS in descending order. Save the query as **Lastname Firstname 3E Staff 7 or More Yrs**

12 Revise the query to answer the question: *Which DR and PM have more than 7 years of service?* Sort by SERV YRS in descending order and SALARY in descending order. Save the query as **Lastname Firstname 3E DR and PM More Than 7 Yrs** and then close the query.

(Project 3E Firefighter Certification Database continues on the next page)

Fire Science

GO! Make It | Project **3E** Firefighter Certification Database (continued)

13 Create a query using both tables that shows EMP ID, LAST NAME, FIRST NAME, RNK, DRIVER/OPERATOR, EMT BASIC, and EMT CPR in that order. Answer the following question: *Which firefighters have all three DRIVER/OPERATOR, EMT BASIC, and EMT CPR certifications?* Sort by LAST NAME in ascending order. Save the query as **Lastname Firstname 3E DR EMT** and then close the query.

14 Create a query that shows the EMP ID, LAST NAME, FIRST NAME, RNK, SERV YRS, and SALARY. Create a calculated field **RAISE** that shows a 3.5% raise by multiplying the SALARY by 3.5%. Then create another calculated field **NEW SALARY** that shows the new salary amount by adding the SALARY and RAISE fields. Format the new fields in Currency. Sort by LAST NAME in ascending order. Change the Page Layout to Landscape. Apply Best Fit to all columns. Save the query as **Lastname Firstname 3E New Salaries** and then close the query.

15 Create a report using the Report Wizard based on the Lastname Firstname 3E New Salaries query. Do not include the FIRST NAME field. Do not Group. Sort by LAST NAME in ascending order. Use the Tabular Layout and Landscape Orientation. Save the report as **Lastname Firstname 3E New Salaries** Modify the report in Layout view. Delete the EMP ID field. Widen and reposition the fields so that the report looks good and all data is visible on one page. Center the column headings. Center the data in all the columns except LAST NAME. Save and close the report.

16 Close the database and submit as directed.

End **You have completed Project 3E**

74 **Access** | Chapter 3: Discipline-Specific Assignments

Fire Science

Apply the skills from these objectives:

1. Create a Table and Define Fields in a New Blank Database
2. Change the Structure of Tables and Add a Second Table
3. Create and Use a Form to Add and Delete Records
4. Create Table Relationships
5. Create a Query in Design View
6. Sort Query Results
7. Specify Criteria in a Query
8. Specify Numeric Criteria in a Query
9. Use Compound Criteria
10. Use Calculated Fields in a Query
11. Calculate Statistics and Group Data in a Query
12. Create a Report by Using the Blank Report Tool or the Report Wizard
13. Modify the Design of a Report
14. Save and Close a Database

GO! Think | Project 3F Fire Science Inspections Database

Project Files

For Project 3F, you will need the following files:

New blank Access database
a3F_Apartment_Buildings (Excel file)
a3F_Inspection_Report (Word file)

You will save your database as:

Lastname_Firstname_3F_Commercial_Inspections

You have been asked to create a new database to store information related to fire inspections of commercial buildings. You will begin with data previously collected during apartment building inspections. You will create a new blank database, create a table based on forms used during an inspection, import data from Excel to create a second table, create a form, create a relationship between the two tables, run queries, and create a report.

1. Create a new blank database and save it to your Fire Science Access folder. Name the database **Lastname_Firstname_3F_Commercial_Inspections**

2. Locate and open **a3F_Inspection_Report**. Look at the information in this Word document, which was completed during an inspection. Data from five different inspections are recorded in this document.

3. In the Lastname_Firstname_3F_Commercial_Inspections database, create a new table to store the a3F_Inspection_Report data beginning with the Business ID. NOTE: The business name and address information in the gray shaded area will be stored in a different table and should not be included in this table.

4. Name the table **Lastname Firstname 3F Inspection Report**

5. Decide which field should be the primary key field. Set the data type to Number for the fields with numbers and Date/Time for the inspection date field.

6. Create a form for the Lastname Firstname 3F Inspection Report, and then save the form with the default name. Using the form, type the inspection data for the five apartment buildings. If a field is empty, leave it blank.

7. Addresses, phone numbers, and contacts for several apartment buildings are saved in an Excel file named **a3F_Apartment_Buildings**. Rather than typing the data, import the **a3F_Apartment _Buildings** Excel worksheet into your new database. Use the first row as column headings, and then choose the primary key field. Save and name the table using the default name.

8. Open both tables, and then size all the columns in each table to Best Fit. Save and close the tables.

9. Create a relationship between the two tables using the field that is common to both tables. Do not enforce referential integrity. Save the relationship.

10. Create a relationship report, and then save it with the default name.

11. Close the report and any open objects.

Access | Chapter 3

(Project 3F Fire Science Inspections Database continues on the next page)

Project 3F: Fire Science Inspections Database | **Access**   75

GO! Think | Project **3F** Fire Science Inspections Database (continued)

12 Create, name, and save queries to answer the following questions. Select fields from both tables or another query when necessary to retrieve the correct data.

- What is the name, street address, and city for each apartment building? Who is the contact person for each building, and what is the phone number? Display them in alphabetical order by business name.

- What are the business names, business IDs, and addresses of the apartments located in the city of Fountain?

- What are the business names, business IDs, and contact persons of those buildings that do not have Knox Equipment? Use the Is Null criteria.

- What are the business IDs, business names, and addresses of those apartments inspected by Montoya? Sort by business ID.

- What are the business names and addresses of those buildings with Metal Frame wall construction and more than one story?

- What are the business IDs and business names of apartment buildings that have more than 20 units per building?

- What are the business IDs and phone numbers of those apartments that were inspected between March and June, and who was the inspector? Sort by inspector.

- What is the approximate total square footage for each apartment building based on the number of units and the average square foot per unit?

13 Based on both tables, create a report that displays the business IDs, business name, inspection date, inspector name, and violations. Group and sort the records as you desire. Widen and reposition columns so that all data is visible. Save the report with the default name. Close the report and any open objects.

14 Save and close the database. Submit it as directed.

End **You have completed Project 3F**

Paralegal

Apply the skills from these objectives:

1. Create a Table and Define Fields in a New Blank Database
2. Change the Structure of Tables and Add a Second Table
3. Create and Use a Form to Add and Delete Records
4. Create Table Relationships
5. Create a Query in Design View
6. Sort Query Results
7. Specify Criteria in a Query
8. Specify Numeric Criteria in a Query
9. Use Compound Criteria
10. Use Wildcards in a Query
11. Use Calculated Fields in a Query
12. Calculate Statistics and Group Data in a Query
13. Create a New Query from an Existing Query
14. Create a Query Based on More Than One Table
15. Create a Report by Using the Blank Report Tool or the Report Wizard
16. Modify the Design of a Report
17. Save and Close a Database

GO! Make It | Project 3G Paralegal Caseload Database

Project Files

For Project 3G, you will need the following files:

New blank Access database
a3G_Paralegal_Caseload (Excel file)

You will save your database as:

Lastname_Firstname_3G_Paralegal_Caseload

Project Results

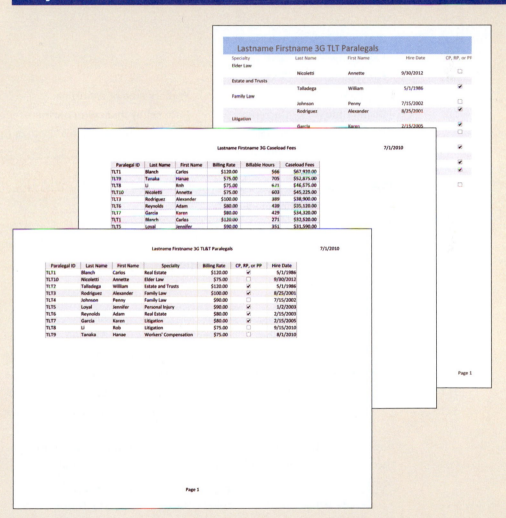

Figure 3.4
Project 3G Paralegal Caseload Database

(Project 3G Paralegal Caseload Database continues on the next page)

GO! Make It | Project 3G Paralegal Caseload Database (continued)

In this database project, you will create a new database to track the paralegal caseload in a large law firm. You will create a table, import data from Excel to create a second table, create forms, add data, create a relationship between the two tables, run queries, and create a report.

1 Create a new folder to store your Access files in, and then name the folder **Paralegal Access**

2 Create a new blank database, and then save it in your Paralegal Access folder. Name the database **Lastname_Firstname_3G_Paralegal_Caseload**

3 Create a table to store general information on the paralegals employed by your firm. Create the following fields, and then name the table **Lastname Firstname 3G TL&T Paralegals**

Field Name	Data type	Description
ID	AutoNumber	
Last Name	Text	
First Name	Text	
Specialty	Text	Primary area of expertise
Billing Rate	Currency	Rate set by managing partners
CP, RP, or PP	Yes/No	Check if Certified, Registered, or Professional
Hire Date	Date/Time	

4 Rename the ID field **Paralegal ID** and then change the data type to text. Set the Paralegal ID field as the primary key field.

5 Change the field properties for the Paralegal ID field to 5, and then set the properties for Billing Rate to be formatted with two decimal places. Save the changes.

6 In Datasheet view, add records for the five paralegals listed below, and then save and close the table.

Paralegal ID	Last Name	First Name	Specialty	Billing Rate	CP, RP, or PP	Hire Date
TLT1	Blanch	Carlos	Real Estate	$120.00	Yes	5/1/1986
TLT2	Talladega	William	Estate and Trusts	$120.00	Yes	5/1/1986
TLT3	Rodriguez	Alexander	Family Law	$100.00	Yes	8/25/2001
TLT4	Johnson	Penny	Family Law	$90.00	No	7/15/2002
TLT5	Loyal	Jennifer	Personal Injury	$90.00	Yes	1/2/2003

7 Create a form for this table, and then accept the default name. Switch to Form view, and then use the form to add the following data for five paralegals:

TLT6	TLT7	TLT8
Reynolds, Adam	Garcia, Karen	Li, Rob
Real Estate	Litigation	Litigation
$80.00	$80.00	$75.00
Yes (Certified CP)	Yes (Certified RP)	Not certified
2/15/2003	2/15/2005	9/15/2010

(Project 3G Paralegal Caseload Database continues on the next page)

GO! Make It | Project 3G Paralegal Caseload Database (continued)

TLT9 Tanaka, Hanae Workers' Compensation $75.00 Not certified 8/1/2010	**TLT10** Nicoletti, Annette Elder Law $75.00 Not certified 9/30/2012

8 Close all open objects.

9 Import the Excel workbook named **a3G_Paralegal_Caseload** into this open database. Use the first row as column headings, and then select the option for no primary key. Name the table **Lastname Firstname 3G Paralegal Caseload**

10 Ensure that the Billable Hours field has a Number data type.

11 Create a form for this table, and then accept the default name.

12 Switch to Form view, and then use the form to add two cases to the database:

Assign paralegal Li, **TLT8** to the following case: Case Number: **WC6754** Case Name: **Martinez vs. Bear Mountain Mining** Client Name: **Martinez, Carl** Billable Hours: **0** Date Opened: **7/14/2012** Date Closed: (leave blank)	Assign paralegal Garcia, **TLT7** to the following case: Case Number: **BR8779** Case Name: **Sopko vs. National Savings & Loan** Client Name: **Sopko, Kay** Billable Hours: **0** Date Opened: **7/15/2012** Date Closed: (leave blank)

13 Save, accept the default form name, and then close the form. Open both tables, and then size all of the columns in each table to Best Fit. Verify that the data entered using the forms are displayed in the tables. Save and close the tables.

14 Create a one-to-many relationship between the two tables using the Paralegal ID field. Enforce referential integrity. Save the relationship.

15 Create a relationship report, and then save it with the default name.

16 Close the report and any open objects.

17 Create the following queries based on one table, both tables, or another query:

- Based on the Lastname Firstname 3G TL&T Paralegals table, create a query that shows Paralegal ID, Last Name, Specialty, and Hire Date. Sort by Hire Date in ascending order. Set the criteria to display those with a Real Estate specialty. Run the query, and then save it as **Lastname Firstname 3G Real Estate Specialty** Close the query.

- Based on the Lastname Firstname 3G TL&T Paralegals table, create a query that shows Last Name, Billing Rate, and CP, RP, or PP. Set the criteria to display those that have a Billing Rate of $90 or higher and a check in the CP, RP, or PP field indicating yes, they have a type of certification. Sort by Billing Rate in descending order. Set the properties for the Billing Rate field to zero decimal places. Run the query, and then save it as **Lastname Firstname 3G Certified and $90 or Higher Rate** Close the query.

(Project 3G Paralegal Caseload Database continues on the next page)

Access | Chapter 3

GO! Make It | Project 3G Paralegal Caseload Database (continued)

- Based on the Lastname Firstname 3G TL&T Paralegals table, create a query that shows Last Name, First Name, Specialty, and Hire Date. Set the criteria to display those that were hired between 1/2/2002 and 12/31/2005. Sort by Hire Date in ascending order. Run the query, and then save it as **Lastname Firstname Hired 2002-2005** Close the query.

- Based on the Lastname Firstname 3G Paralegal Caseload table, create a query that shows Paralegal ID, Case Number, Case Name, Date Opened, and Date Closed. Use a wildcard with criteria in the Case Number field to display only Estate Trust and Elder Law cases, which will have case numbers that begin with the letter E. Sort by Date Opened in ascending order. Run the query, and then save it as **Lastname Firstname 3G Estate Trust and Elder Law Cases** Close the query.

- Based on the Lastname Firstname 3G Paralegal Caseload table, create a query that shows Case Number, Case Name, Client Last Name, Date Opened, and Date Closed. Use the Is Null criteria to display the cases that do not have a Date Closed date. Sort by the Date Opened field in ascending order. Clear the Show check box for the Date Closed field. Run the query, and then save it as **Lastname Firstname 3G Open Cases** Close the query.

- Create a query based on both tables. From the Lastname Firstname 3G TL&T Paralegals table, show the Paralegal ID, Last Name, First Name, and Billing Rate. From the Lastname Firstname 3G Paralegal Caseload table, show the Billable Hours field. Create a field **Caseload Fees** to calculate the caseload fees by multiplying the Billing Rate by the Billable Hours. Set the properties for the Caseload Fees field to Currency with two decimal places. Sort by Caseload Fees in descending order. Run the query, and then save it as **Lastname Firstname 3G Caseload Fees** Close the query.

- Based on the Lastname Firstname 3G Caseload Fees query, create a query to total the Caseload Fees by Last Name using the Total row. Set the properties for Caseload Fees to Currency with zero decimal places. Run the query, and then save it as **Lastname Firstname 3G Total Caseload Fees** Close the query.

18 Using the Report Wizard, create a report based on the Lastname Firstname 3G TL&T Paralegals table. Include the Last Name, First Name, Specialty, Hire Date, and CP, RP, and PP fields. Group by Specialty, sort by Last Name in ascending order, and accept the Stepped and Portrait default settings. Finish creating the report, and then modify the report in Layout view. Resize and reposition columns so that all data is visible and evenly spaced. If necessary, reposition the page number in the footer so that it is visible. Save the report with the default name, and then close it.

19 Save the database and submit it as directed.

End You have completed Project 3G ————————————————

Paralegal

GO! Think | Project 3H Legal Stockholders Database

Project Files

For Project 3H, you will need the following files:

a3H_Legal_Stocks (Excel File)
a3H_Legal_Stockholders (Access file)

You will save your database as:

Lastname_Firstname_3H_Legal_Stockholders

In this database project, you will work with a database of stockholders. You will import a table of stocks from Excel to create a second table, create forms, add data, create a relationship between the two tables, create and run queries, and create a report.

1 From the student files that accompany this textbook, open **a3H_Legal_Stockholders**, and then save it to your Paralegal Access folder as **Lastname_Firstname_3H_Legal_Stockholders** Enable the content. Open the **3H Stockholders** table. Apply Best Fit to all columns. Save the table.

2 Create a table by importing the **a3H_Legal_Stocks** workbook, use the first row as column headings, and use the ID field as the primary key. Name the table **Lastname Firstname 3H Legal Stocks** After the table is imported in to Access, delete the Last Name and First Name fields and apply Best Fit to all columns. Format both Shares fields as a Standard number with a comma and no decimals. Save and close the table. Ensure that objects on the Navigation Pane are grouped by Tables and Related Views. Be sure that all object names display fully.

3 Create a one-to-one relationship between the two tables using the ID field. Enforce referential integrity. Create a relationship report and save it with the default name. Close the report and the relationship.

4 Open both tables. Because you have created a relationship, you will see the plus sign or expand symbol to the left of each record. When you click on the plus sign in the Lastname Firstname 3H Legal Stocks table, you will see the stockholders' information. In the 3H Stockholders table, you will see the stock information for each record. Close the tables.

5 Create a form for the 3H Stockholders table, and then accept the default name. Add the following two new stockholders.

ID: **13-1876**	ID: **13-1877**
Marta Washington	**Wally Asterisk**
2899 West Colorado	**1735 Big Oak Drive**
Colorado Springs, CO 80903	**Colorado Springs, CO 80919**
Call me during the day? **Yes**	Call me during the day? **No**
Day phone: **719-555-5534**	Day phone: **719-555-2389**
Call me in the evening? **No**	Call me in the evening? **Yes**
Evening Phone: **719-555-2234**	Evening Phone: **719-555-3899**
E-mail me? **Yes**	E-mail me? **Yes**
E-mail address: **mwashing2@url.com**	E-mail address: **asteriskwa@url.com**

(Project 3H Legal Stockholders Database continues on the next page)

Access | Chapter 3

GO! Think | Project 3H Legal Stockholders Database (continued)

6 Create a form for the Lastname Firstname 3H Legal Stocks table, and then accept the default name. Add the following two new records to the table.

> ID: **13-1876**
> Common Shares: **182000**
> Series A Preferred Shares: **0**
>
> ID: **13-1877**
> Common Shares: **125000**
> Series A Preferred Shares: **0**

7 Create the following queries. Show all pertinent data.

- Create a query that answers the question: *Which stockholder has both Common Stock and Series A Preferred Stock greater than 0?* Save and close the query.

- Create a query that answers the question: *Which stockholders prefer to be called anytime?* Sort by Last Name in ascending order. Save and close the query.

- Create a query that answers the question: *Which stockholders have 0 common shares?* Sort by Last Name in ascending order. Save and close the query.

- Edit the Stockholders with 0 common shares query to show stockholders with Series A Preferred Stock only. Sort by Last Name in ascending order. Save and close the query.

- Create a query that answers the question: *Which stockholders have Series A Preferred Stock >25,000?* Sort by Series A Preferred Shares in descending order. Save and close the query.

- Create a query using the SUM function that answers the question: *What is the total number of Common Shares and what is the total number of Series A Preferred Shares?* Format each result as a Standard number with no decimals. Save and close the query.

- Create a query using both tables. Include the Last Name, First Name, Common Shares, and Series A Preferred Shares. Create a calculated field **Total Shares** that shows the total Common and Series A Preferred Shares. Format the Total Shares field as a Standard number with no decimals. Save and close the query.

8 Create a report based on the Total Shares query that shows Last Name, First Name, Common Shares, Series A Preferred Shares, and Total Shares. Sort in ascending order by Last Name. Modify the report in Layout view, and then ensure that the columns are evenly spaced on the page and all information is visible. Save and close the report.

9 Close the database and submit it as directed.

End **You have completed Project 3H**

Discipline-Specific Assignments

You will complete the following discipline-specific projects:

| CULINARY ARTS | GO! Make It | Project 4A Community Garden (p. 84)
GO! Think | Project 4B Healthy Recipe (p. 88) |

| DENTAL ASSISTING | GO! Make It | Project 4C Teeth Whitening (p. 89)
GO! Think | Project 4D Dental Office (p. 92) |

| FIRE SCIENCE | GO! Make It | Project 4E Fire Training (p. 93)
GO! Think | Project 4F Wildfire Prevention (p. 97) |

| PARALEGAL | GO! Make It | Project 4G Jury Selection (p. 99)
GO! Think | Project 4H Community Presentation (p. 102) |

Culinary Arts

GO! Make It | Project **4A** Community Garden

Project Files

For Project 4A, you will need the following files:

p4A_Community_Garden
p4A_Chef
p4A_Club_Logo
p4A_Garden
p4A_Hands
p4A_Garden_Photo
p4A_Grass

p4A_Mr._Tomato
p4A_PPCC_Logo
p4A_Smiley_Face
p4A_Tomato
p4A_Vegetables
p4A_Vegetables_2
p4A_Veggie_Tree

You will save your presentation as:

Lastname_Firstname_4A_Community_Garden

Project Results

Figure 4.1

(Project 4A Community Garden continues on the next page)

Culinary Arts

You are a culinary student and your culinary arts club has created a community garden. You have been asked to create a presentation for another school to give students more information about your project.

Create a new folder to store your PowerPoint files in, and then name the folder **Culinary Arts PowerPoint** From the student files that accompany this textbook, locate and open the file **p4A_Community_Garden**, and then save the file in your PowerPoint folder as **Lastname_Firstname_4A_Community_Garden**

Create the presentation by completing the following steps:

1 On Slide 1, create a WordArt title with Fill – Dark Green, Accent 1, Metal Bevel, Reflection Style, and then type the text **Community Garden** Change the background style graphics for the title slide to picture, and then insert the **p4A_Grass** picture as the background. In the upper left corner of the slide, insert the **p4A_PPCC_Logo** picture. Size it 1.4" high and 2" wide. In the upper right corner of the slide, insert the **p4A_Club_Logo** picture. Size it 2" high by 1.2" wide. Select both pictures at the top of the slide, and then apply Wheel Entrance Animation with the One Spoke Effect Option. In the lower right corner of the grass, insert the **p4A_Mr._Tomato** picture. Size it 1.9" high by 1.82" wide. Select the **p4A_Mr._Tomato** picture, and then apply the Teeter Emphasis Animation. Move the WordArt Title up on the slide as shown in Figure 4.1, and then center it horizontally on the slide.

2 Insert a new slide with the Title Only layout. In the title placeholder, type **Purpose** Draw a text box in the middle of the slide, and then type the following information:

Provide an educational opportunity for PPCC Culinary Arts students to cultivate green space and promote awareness of the environment, health, and nutrition among students, faculty, and staff.

3 Change the font to 28 pt, and then center the text in the box. Size the box 2.2" high by 8.1" wide. Change the shape style to Colored Fill – Dark Green, Accent 1. Align the box in the center and middle of the slide. Change the Shape Effects to Reflection, Half Reflection, touching. Apply the Fly In From Bottom Entrance Animation to the text box. In the upper right corner of the slide, insert the **p4A_Hands** picture. Size it 2.0" high by 1.79" wide. Select the picture, and then apply the Fly In From Top-Right Entrance Animation. Reorder the animation so the picture animation comes before the text box animation.

4 Insert a new slide with Title and Content layout. In the title placeholder, type **Goals** Create a SmartArt Continuous Picture List with the following information:

- Type **Promote Healthy Life Style** in the left column, and then insert the **p4A_Vegetables** picture.
- Type **Promote Awareness** in the center column, and then insert the **p4A_Tomato** picture.
- Type **Provide Help for Students** in the right column, and then insert the **p4A_Vegetables_2** picture.

5 Format the arrow shape at the bottom of the SmartArt with Standard Color Orange fill. Center the SmartArt. Select the SmartArt, and then apply the Fade Entrance Animation with the As One Object Effect Option. On the Notes pane, type the following note:

A community garden will promote awareness of the impact WE have on OUR environment. It will also provide for the many needs of the students in the PPCC community.

(Project 4A Community Garden continues on the next page)

PowerPoint | Chapter 4

GO! Make It | Project **4A** Community
Garden (continued)

6 Insert a new slide with the Title and Content layout. In the title placeholder, type **Benefits and Rewards** Use a bulleted list and type the following information:

> **Develop a program for storing, processing, and composting waste.**
>
> **Use composted soil for on-site gardens and greenhouse.**
>
> **Reduce food costs for the PPCC culinary program.**
>
> **Promote public relations in the PPCC community.**

7 Convert the bulleted text into a Vertical Bullet List SmartArt. Change the color of the SmartArt to Colored Fill – Accent 2. Change the SmartArt Style to 3-D Metallic Scene. Center the SmartArt. In the upper right corner of the slide, insert the **p4A_Smiley_Face** picture. Size the picture 1.6" high by 1.87" wide. Apply the Drop Shadow Rectangle Picture Style. Apply the Fly In From Top Right Entrance Animation to the picture. Select the SmartArt, and then apply the Fade Entrance Animation with the One by One Effect Option.

8 Insert four new slides from the **p4A_Garden** presentation. Reuse all four slides by right-clicking on a slide, and then selecting Insert All Slides.

9 On the first new slide, Slide 5, change the text *Green* to 32 pt Standard Green, bold, and small caps.

10 On the second new slide, Slide 6, edit the Smart Art pyramid color to Colored Fill – Accent 2. Change the SmartArt style to 3-D Inset. Add a fourth text box shape after the last one, and then type **Manitou Castle** Select the SmartArt, and then apply the Fade Entrance Animation with the One by One Effect Option. On the left of the slide, insert the **p4A_Chef** picture. Size the picture 2" high by 1.5" wide. Draw a Rounded Rectangular Callout as shown in Figure 4.1. In the callout, type **We support PPCC!** Size the text to 24 pt.

11 On Slide 7, select the SmartArt, and then apply the Fly In From Left Entrance Animation with the One by One Effect Option.

12 In Slide 8, insert the **p4A_Veggie_Tree** picture to the right of the bulleted text. Size the picture 4.5" high and 2.72" wide. Apply the picture style Bevel Perspective Left, White. Apply the Grow and Turn Entrance Animation.

13 Insert a new slide with Title and Content layout, and then title it **Financial Contributors**

14 Insert a table with the following information:

Organization	Amount
PPCC Foundation	$1,500
Student Government	3,000
Culinary Arts Club	500
Community and Business Donations	1,000
Total	$6,000

15 Apply the Table Style Dark Style 1 – Accent 1. Change the font for the entire table to 28 pt. Center the column headings. Right-align the dollar amounts. Size the first column 6" wide. Size the second column 3" wide. Size the table 4.8" high. Center the table horizontally on the slide. Vertically center text within the cells of the table. Change the font for Total and $6,000 to 32 pt bold. Select the table, and then apply Fade Entrance Animation.

(Project 4A Community Garden continues on the next page)

GO! Make It | Project **4A** Community Garden (continued)

16 Select Slides 2 through 9. Change the background style for all of the selected slides to a picture by using the **p4A_Grass** picture. In the Format Background dialog box, edit the picture's Offsets in Stretch options, so the dimensions are 0% for the top and −40% for the bottom. This places the grass picture at the bottom of each slide, but it is not as high as on Slide 1.

17 After Slide 9, insert a new slide with Picture with Caption layout.

18 Insert the **p4A_Garden_Photo** picture. Apply the Zoom Entrance Animation with the Object Center Effect Option. Format the background style to Solid Fill Standard Green color. In the upper left corner of the slide, insert the **p4A_PPCC_Logo** picture. Size it 1.4" high by 2" wide. Apply the Reflected Perspective Right Picture Style. Type the title **PPCC Community Garden Completed June 2012** and then bold the text. Apply the Split Entrance Animation with the Horizontal Out Effect Option. Under the title caption, type **For further information, contact the Culinary Arts Department at Pikes Peak Community College.** Size the text in the bottom placeholder to 22 pt, and then bold and center it. Apply the Split Entrance Animation with the Horizontal Out Effect Option.

19 Apply the Transition Cover with the From Right Effect Option to all slides.

20 Insert a header and footer for the Notes and Handouts. Display a date that updates automatically. Add the page number and **Presented by Firstname Lastname** to the footer. Insert the slide number on each slide but do not include it on the title slide.

21 Run the slide show and proofread. Change the print settings so the presentation is printed as Handouts (3 slides per page). Save the presentation and submit it as directed.

End You have completed Project 4A —————————————————

GO! Think | Project 4B Healthy Recipe

Project Files

For Project 4B, you will need the following file:

New blank PowerPoint presentation

You will save your presentation as:

Lastname_Firstname_4B_Healthy_Recipe

Create a new blank PowerPoint presentation file. Save the file in the Culinary Arts PowerPoint chapter folder as **Lastname_Firstname_4B_Healthy_Recipe**

Your culinary arts club is participating in a neighborhood health fair, and you have been asked to create a PowerPoint presentation for general public viewing. The purpose of the presentation is to explain how to prepare a healthy recipe. Visit the government-sponsored Web sites listed below or search the Internet for a recipe. Keep in mind that you should cite your source(s) in your presentation. Copyrighted recipes or photos should be used only if permission is granted.

Some suggested Web sites for researching recipes are:

- http://www.smallstep.gov/eb/recipes.html
- http://www.FruitsandVeggiesMatter.gov
- http://www.nutrition.gov
- http://www.cdc.gov/healthyweight/healthy_eating/recipes.html

The content of your presentation should include a list of ingredients, preparation directions, a photo of the finished recipe, and nutritional information such as calories, fat, cholesterol, fiber, protein, and carbohydrates.

As you prepare your slides, follow these guidelines:

1 Apply a theme of your choice.

2 Use three different slide layouts.

3 Insert clip art or a photo on at least one slide that is related to your topic. Apply a picture style and picture effects.

4 Insert SmartArt on at least one slide, change colors, and apply a style.

5 Apply transitions to all slides and animations to three or more slides.

6 Insert the following footer on the slides: **Presented by Firstname Lastname** Insert a header on the Notes and Handouts that displays the name of your presentation, display a date that updates automatically, and then add a footer that displays the file name.

7 Apply a background style and hide graphics if appropriate.

8 Use WordArt on at least one slide.

9 Apply bullets and/or numbering on at least one slide.

10 Create a table to display information about your recipe.

11 Create a chart and animate it to display data such as nutritional information.

12 Insert a text box or a shape to one or more slides.

13 In the Notes pane, insert notes about the points you plan to make during the presentation.

14 Run the slide show and proofread. Change the print settings so that the presentation is printed as Notes Pages. Save the presentation and submit it as directed.

 You have completed Project 4B ——————————————

Dental Assisting

GO! Make It | Project 4C Teeth Whitening

Project Files

For Project 4C, you will need the following files:

p4C_Teeth_Whitening
p4C_Whitening_Treatments
p4C_Blueberries
p4C_Cigarettes

p4C_Calendar
p4C_Coffee
p4C_Rx

You will save your presentation as:

Lastname_Firstname_4C_Teeth_Whitening

Project Results

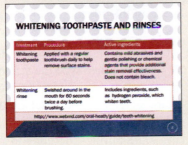

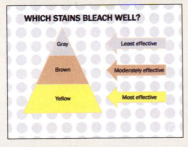
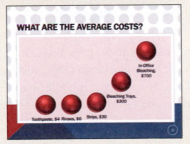

Figure 4.2

(Project 4C Teeth Whitening continues on the next page)

GO! Make It | Project **4C** Teeth Whitening (continued)

Create a new chapter folder to store your PowerPoint files, and then name the folder **Dental Assisting PowerPoint** From the student files that accompany this textbook, locate and open the file **p4C_Teeth_Whitening**, and then save the file in the Dental Assisting PowerPoint folder as **Lastname_Firstname_4C_Teeth_Whitening**

This presentation will be used to educate patients who might want to use a teeth-whitening treatment.

Modify the presentation file as follows:

1 Apply the Angles theme to all slides. Select Aspect as the theme color.

2 After Slide 2, reuse all four slides from **p4C_Whitening_Treatments**.

3 Add a footer that displays the slide number to all slides, except the title slide. Add a header to all pages of the Notes and Handouts that displays the text **Teeth Whitening Patient Guide** Add a footer to all pages of the Notes and Handouts that displays the text **Lastname Firstname 4C Teeth Whitening** and a date that updates automatically.

4 Apply Background Style 9 and the Clock transition to all slides.

5 On Slide 2, in the content placeholder, convert the five lines of text to a Horizontal Picture List SmartArt graphic. Size the graphic to 3.5" high by 9.25" wide, and then center it on the slide. Change the SmartArt graphic colors to Colorful Range – Accent Colors 2 to 3, and then apply the 3-D Polished style. Insert **p4C_Calendar**, **p4C_Blueberries**, **p4C_Rx**, **p4C_Cigarettes**, and **p4C_Coffee** as shown in Figure 4.2. In the title placeholder, increase the font size to 36 pt.

6 Use Format Painter to apply the font effects of the title text on Slide 2 to the title text on all slides except the first and last slide.

7 On Slide 3, change the slide layout to Title Only, and then insert a Flowchart: Magnetic Disk shape. Size the shape to 3" high by 2.65" wide, and then type the text **Whitening Toothpastes and Rinses** inside the shape. Increase the font size of the text to 32 pt. Copy the shape two times, and then type the text **At-Home Bleaching** and **In-Office Bleaching** inside the two shapes. Align the three objects in the middle and distribute horizontally so they will be evenly spaced. Apply Shape Style Colored Fill – Dark Purple – Accent 5 to the left shape, Colored Fill – Dark Blue – Accent 3 to the middle shape, and Colored Fill – Red – Accent 2 to the right shape.

8 On Slides 4 and 5, apply Table Style Medium Style 1 – Accent 2 to the existing tables. Add a row to the bottom of each table, and then change the row height to .5 Merge the cells in the last row, and then type in the following URL: **http://www.webmd.com/oral-health/guide/teeth-whitening** Center align the text in the last row of each table. Size the tables to 4.5" high by 9" wide.

9 On Slide 6, insert a 3 column, 3 row table. Merge the cells in the last row, and then change the row height to .5 Type the text below:

Treatment	Procedure	Active Ingredients
In-Office Bleaching	Applied directly to the teeth. Can be used in combination with heat, a special light, and/or a laser.	Peroxide bleaching agent
	Results seen in one treatment	
http://www.webmd.com/oral-health/guide/teeth-whitening		

(Project 4C Teeth Whitening continues on the next page)

Dental Assisting

GO! Make It | Project **4C** Teeth Whitening (continued)

10 On Slide 6, apply Table Style Medium Style 1 – Accent 2 to the table. Size the table to 3.75" high by 9" wide, and then center it on the slide. Center the text in the bottom row.

11 Refer to Figure 4.2, and on Slide 7, apply Shape Fill Gray-80%, Text 2, Lighter 75% to the top section of the pyramid; apply Tan, Accent 6, Lighter 40% to the middle section; and apply Light Yellow, which is found in More Fill Colors—Standard tab, third from center, to the bottom section. Apply the same fill color to the corresponding arrow shape as previously applied to the pyramid. Arrange the pyramid and the three arrow shapes on the slide so that arrows are aligned and point to corresponding shade on the pyramid. Hide the background graphics on the slide.

12 On Slide 8, create a Bubble chart with a 3-D effect. In the Excel worksheet that opens, type the data shown below. Delete the Size row.

X-Values	Y-Values
Toothpaste	**$4**
Rinses	**$6**
Strips	**$30**
Bleaching Trays	**$300**
In-Office Bleaching	**$700**

13 Apply chart style 36. Change the chart layout by applying a None setting to the Chart Title, Axis Titles, Legend, Axes, and Gridlines. Change the Data Labels Options to contain the X and Y value and the Label Position to Below. Resize the chart to 5" high by 9" wide, and then center the chart on the slide so that the title text is visible. In the Notes pane, type **Average fees charged by local providers**

14 On Slide 9, convert the four lines of text to a Stacked List SmartArt graphic. In the Text pane, promote and demote the text so that the text *Teeth Sensitivity* and *Gum Irritation* displays in the circles and the remaining text displays in the rectangles. Size the graphic to 3.5" high by 8" wide, and then center it on the slide. Change the SmartArt graphic colors to Colorful – Accent Colors, and then apply the 3-D Inset style. Animate the SmartArt with a Zoom Entrance, and then set Effect Options to a Level at Once sequence.

15 At the bottom of Slide 9, insert WordArt Fill - Red, Accent 2, Matte Bevel with the text **Talk to your dentist about what is best for you!** And then position it at the bottom center of the slide. Change the font size to 44, and then break the text into two lines. Size the WordArt to 1.75" high by 7.25" wide. Apply Shape Style Colored Outline - Red, Accent 2 to the WordArt. Position the objects and text on the slide so that they are evenly spaced on the slide. In the Notes pane, type **Primary sources of information: American Dental Association and WebMd.com** Animate the WordArt with a Zoom entrance and ensure that it displays after the SmartArt.

16 Find and replace text At Home with **At-Home** and In Office with **In-Office**. Run the slide show and proofread. Run the slide show and proofread. Change the print settings so that the presentation is printed as Handouts (3 slides per page). Save the presentation and submit it as directed.

 You have completed Project 4C ——————————

Dental Assisting

GO! Think | Project **4D** Dental Office

Project Files

For Project 4D, you will need the following file:

New blank PowerPoint presentation

You will save your presentation as:

Lastname_Firstname_4D_Dental_Office

Start PowerPoint, and open a new blank presentation. Save the file in your Dental Assisting PowerPoint folder as **Lastname_Firstname_4D_Dental_Office**

Dental assistants work at many different types of offices. If you were to pick the perfect dental office, what would it be like? Where would it be located? How large would the office be? What procedures and services would be offered?

Use the Internet to research dental offices to learn about what kinds of services they provide. Determine what dental procedures your office will offer. Examples are implants, cosmetic dentistry, sedation, general procedures, and restorative procedures. Create a name for your office that reflects your services and atmosphere. Create a PowerPoint presentation that includes office information and services offered.

Your presentation should summarize the information and show prospective patients why they should come to your office. Cite source(s) used in your presentation when needed. Include the following:

1 Apply an appropriate theme and theme color.

2 Apply a background style.

3 Keep bulleted slides to a maximum of two. Customize the bullets on the bulleted slides. Follow the 6 × 6 rule. (No more than 6 lines of text and no more than 6 words in a line.)

4 Use SmartArt on at least three slides. Apply animation to the SmartArt objects.

5 Use at least one table or chart and animate the table or chart.

6 Determine the location of your office and use MapQuest to get a map. Right-click on the map, save the picture, and then insert it on one of your slides. Animate the picture.

7 Use clip art or a photo on at least two slides. Apply picture styles and picture effects, and apply animation.

8 Use WordArt on at least one slide.

9 Use drawing objects on at least one slide. Add text to the drawing objects. Format the border and fill of the objects. Animate the drawing objects.

10 Apply slide transitions to all slides.

11 Insert notes in the Notes pane of points you plan to make during the presentation.

12 Insert a header and footer for the Notes and Handouts. Include the date and have it automatically update. Add the page number and filename **Lastname_Firstname_4D_Dental_Office** to the footer. Insert the slide number on each slide but do not include it on the title slide.

13 Run the slide show and proofread. Change the print settings so the presentation is printed as Notes Pages. Save the presentation and submit it as directed.

 You have completed Project 4D ——————————————————

Fire Science

GO! Make It | Project 4E Fire Training

Project Files

For Project 4E, you will need the following files:

New blank PowerPoint presentation
p4E_Fire_Inspection
p4E_Station_8
p4E_Key_Lock

p4E_Hazard
p4E_Fire_Hydrant
p4E_No_Parking
p4E_Numbers

You will save your presentation as:

Lastname_Firstname_4E_Fire_Training

Project Results

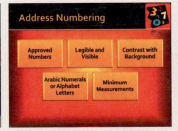

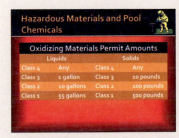

Figure 4.3

(Project 4E Fire Training continues on the next page)

GO! Make It | Project **4E** Fire Training (continued)

Create a new chapter folder to store your PowerPoint files, and then name the folder **Fire Science PowerPoint**

You are a firefighter in Station 8, and you have been asked to create a PowerPoint presentation about fire code inspections to be given to the firefighters at your local station who are in training. This training might also be used at other local stations. Remember that there will be Notes Pages with the detailed information that you will share. The PowerPoint slides should reference the information that you will communicate.

Start PowerPoint and begin a new blank presentation. Apply the Module Built-In theme. Save the file to your PowerPoint folder as **Lastname_Firstname_4E_Fire_Training**

1 On Slide 1, delete the title placeholder. Move the subtitle placeholder to the bottom of the slide. In the subtitle placeholder, type **Fire Inspection Training** Size it to 32 pt, and then apply bold and black. Center the text in the placeholder. Center the placeholder. Hide the Background graphics. Use WordArt, and then type the title **Colorado Springs Fire Department** Apply the Fill – Blue-Gray, Text 2, Outline – Background 2. Change the font to 44 pt and small cap. Move the title to the top of the slide as shown in Figure 4.3. Edit the Background Style, and then insert the **p4E_Station_8** picture as the background of the slide. Be sure the subtitle text is visible at the bottom of the slide.

2 Insert a new slide with the Title and Content layout. In the title placeholder, type **Address Numbering** On the right side of the title in the upper right corner of the slide, insert the **p4E_Numbers** picture. Size the picture 1.55" high by 1.55" wide. Apply the Reflected Rounded Rectangle Picture Style. Animate the picture with the Grow & Turn Entrance Effect.

3 Create a Basic Block List SmartArt that has the following information about address numbering:

Approved Numbers

Legible and Visible

Contrast with Background

Arabic Numerals or Alphabet Letters

Minimum Measurements

4 Change the SmartArt Style to 3-D Inset. Size the SmartArt 5.06" high by 9" wide. Center the SmartArt on the slide. Change the font for the SmartArt to black bold. Animate the SmartArt with the Zoom Entrance Effect with the Object Center and One by One Effect Options. Type **Minimum stroke 5" high and 0.5" wide** in the Notes pane for the slide.

5 Insert a new slide with Title Only layout, and in the title placeholder, type **Knox™ Equipment Keys** Be sure to type the Trademark symbol by using the Insert, Symbol feature. At the right of the title, insert the **p4E_Key_Lock** picture. Size the picture 1.9" high by 1.6" wide, and then position it in the upper right corner of the slide. Apply the Appear Entrance Animation. Insert the Converging Radial Relationship SmartArt. Type the following text in the SmartArt beginning with the left text box:

Access

Fire Protection Systems

Elevators

And in the bottom circle, type **2 Sets Required**

(Project 4E Fire Training continues on the next page)

Fire Science

GO! Make It | Project **4E** Fire Training (continued)

6 Change the SmartArt colors to Colorful Range – Accent Colors 2 to 3. Change the style to 3-D Metallic Scene. Size the SmartArt 5.06" high by 9" wide. Center the SmartArt. Select the SmartArt, and then apply the Fade Entrance Animation with the One by One Effect Option. In the Notes pane for this slide, type the following text:

> **Each box MUST contain at least two sets of labeled keys for access to and through buildings, fire protection systems, and elevators.**

7 Insert a new slide with the Title and Content layout, and then in the title placeholder, type **Fire Hydrants** Insert the following in bulleted text:

> **Inspection, Testing, Maintenance**
>
> **Clear Space – 3 ft. clear circumference**
>
> **Vehicle Parking – 5 ft. clearance**

8 Convert the bulleted text to a Vertical Bullet List SmartArt. Change the SmartArt Style to 3-D Polished. Add a fourth shape **Obstruction** Select the SmartArt, and then apply Fade Entrance Animation with the One by One Effect Option. In the upper right corner of the slide, insert the **p4E_Fire_Hydrant** picture. Size it 1.5" high by 1.5" wide, and then position it as shown in Figure 4.3. Apply the Zoom Entrance Animation. Reorder the animation for the picture so it appears before the SmartArt.

9 Insert new slides by reusing all eight slides from **p4E_Fire_Inspection**. Right-click, and then Insert All Slides into your presentation.

10 On Slide 5, draw a text box above the shapes, and then in the box, type **Access roads shall not be obstructed in any manner including the parking of vehicles!** Bold and center the text in the box. Size the box 1.1" high and 4.7" wide. Change the Shape Style to Intense Effect – Black, Dark 1. Center the text box on the slide. In the upper right corner of the slide, insert the **p4E_No_Parking** picture. Size the picture 1.5" high by 2.2" wide. Apply Grow/Shrink Emphasis Animation to the picture.

11 Move the slide *Fire Alarm and Sprinklers* to be Slide 6. Change the font in the bulleted items to 36 pt bold. Adjust the placeholder for the bulleted items so each one is on one line only.

12 Insert a new slide after Slide 9 with Title and Content layout. In the title, type **Hazardous Materials and Pool Chemicals**

13 On the slide, create the table below, and type the information as shown. Merge the cells in the top row, and then center the title text. Merge columns 1 and 2 in row 2 and merge columns 3 and 4 in row 2, and then center the heading text.

Oxidizing Materials Permit Amounts			
Liquids		Solids	
Class 4	Any	Class 4	Any
Class 3	1 gallon	Class 3	10 pounds
Class 2	10 gallons	Class 2	100 pounds
Class 1	55 gallons	Class 1	500 pounds

(Project 4E Fire Training continues on the next page)

Project 4E: Fire Training | **Powerpoint** 95

GO! Make It | Project **4E** Fire Training (continued)

14 Change the table style to Dark Style 1 – Accent 1. Change the font for the title row in the table to 36 pt. Change the font for the other rows in the table to 28 pt bold. Align the table in the center and middle of the slide. Apply the Shape Entrance Animation with In and Box Effect Options. Insert the **p4E_Hazard** picture in the upper right corner of the slide. Size the picture 1.5" high by 1.51" wide. Apply the Grow & Turn Entrance Animation. Reorder the animation so the picture appears before the table.

15 On Slide 12, select the bulleted text, and then convert the text to a Target List SmartArt. Bold the text in the SmartArt. Select the SmartArt, and then apply the Wheel Entrance Animation with One Spoke and the As One Object Effect Option.

16 Select Slides 2 to 13, and then change the background to Gradient fill, Preset colors, Fire. Change the Gradient type to Path.

17 On Slide 13, draw a text box at the left of the slide. Type the text **For more information, contact CSFD Station 8 at 719-555-1222.** Size the text to 24 pt, and then bold and center the text in the box. Size and position the box so the text fits as shown in Figure 4.3. In the lower left corner of the slide, insert the **p4E_Station_8** picture. Size it 2.35" high by 3.13" wide. Apply the Drop Shadow Rectangle picture effect.

18 Apply the Split Transition with Vertical Out Effect Option to all slides.

19 Insert a header and footer for the Notes and Handouts. Include the date and have it automatically update. Add the page number and filename **Lastname_Firstname_4E_Fire_Training** to the footer.

20 Run the slide show and proofread. Change the print settings so the presentation is printed as Handouts (3 slides per page). Save the presentation and submit it as directed.

End **You have completed Project 4E** _____

Fire Science

GO! Think | Project 4F Wildfire Prevention

Project Files

For Project 4F, you will need the following file:

New blank PowerPoint presentation

You will save your presentation as:

Lastname_Firstname_4F_Wildfire_Prevention

Create a new blank PowerPoint presentation. Save the file in the Fire Science PowerPoint chapter folder as **Lastname_Firstname_4F_Wildfire_Prevention**

Your fire station is hosting an open house for neighborhood residents. Some sections of your service area are susceptible to wildfires. You have been asked to create a PowerPoint presentation for general public viewing. The purpose of the presentation is to explain how individual homeowners can reduce the chance and/or spread of a wildfire and also demonstrate techniques that are used when fighting wildfires. Search the Internet for information. Keep in mind that you should cite your source(s) in your presentation. Copyrighted photos should be used only if permission is granted.

The content of your presentation should include:

- Recent statistics on wildfires
- Methods of fighting wildfires
- Equipment needed
- Firefighter training
- Tips for homeowners on how to reduce the spread of wildfires
- Interagency collaboration
- Some suggested Web sites:

  http://www.fema.gov/hazard/wildfire/index.shtm
  http://www.nifc.gov/
  http://www.fs.fed.us/fire/
  http://www.dola.state.co.us/dem/public_information/wildfire.htm
  http://www.usgs.gov/hazards/wildfires/

As you prepare your slides, follow these guidelines:

1. Choose and apply a theme.
2. Use three different slide layouts.
3. Insert clip art or a photo on at least one slide that is related to your topic. Apply a picture style and picture effects.
4. Insert SmartArt on at least one slide, change colors, and apply a style.
5. Apply animations to three or more slides and transitions to all slides.
6. On all of the slides, insert the footer **Presented by Firstname Lastname** On the Notes and Handouts, insert a header that displays the name of your presentation, display a date that updates automatically, and insert a footer that displays the file name.
7. Apply a background style and hide graphics if appropriate.
8. Use WordArt on at least one slide.
9. Apply bullets and/or numbering on at least one slide.
10. Create a table.

(Project 4F Wildfire Prevention continues on the next page)

GO! Make It | Project **4F** Wildfire Prevention (continued)

11 Create a chart and animate it

12 Insert a text box or a shape to one or more slides.

13 In the Notes pane, insert notes about the points you plan to make during the presentation.

14 Run the slide show and proofread. Change the print settings so that the presentation is printed as Notes Pages. Save the presentation and submit it as directed.

End **You have completed Project 4F** ———————————————————

Apply the skills from these objectives:

1 Edit an Existing Presentation

2 Add Pictures to a Presentation

3 Print and View a Presentation

4 Format a Presentation

5 Apply Slide Transitions

6 Insert Text Boxes and Shapes

7 Format Objects

8 Remove Picture Backgrounds and Insert WordArt

9 Create and Format a SmartArt Graphic

10 Customize Slide Backgrounds and Themes

11 Animate a Slide Show

12 Create and Modify Tables

13 Create and Modify Charts

GO! Make It | Project **4G** Jury Selection

Project Files

For Project 4G, you will need the following files:

p4G_Jury_Selection
p4G_Jury_Qualifications
p4G_Federal_Court

p4G_Jury
p4G_Courtroom

You will save your presentation as:

Lastname_Firstname_4G_Jury_Selection

Project Results

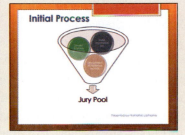
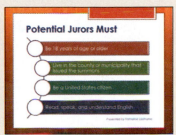
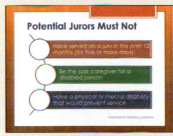
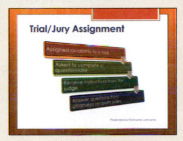
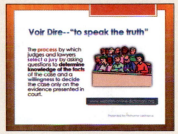

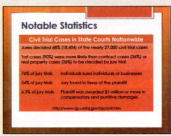
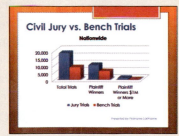
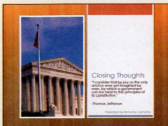

Figure 4.4

(Project 4G Jury Selection continues on the next page)

GO! Make It | Project **4G** Jury Selection (continued)

Create a new folder to store your PowerPoint files in, and then name the folder **Paralegal PowerPoint** From the student files that accompany this textbook, locate and open the file **p4G_Jury_Selection**, and then save the file in the Paralegal PowerPoint folder as **Lastname_Firstname_4G_Jury_Selection**

As a paralegal in a large law firm, you have been asked to prepare a short training presentation on the topic of jury selection.

Apply the Austin theme to all slides, and then change the theme colors to Horizon.

After Slide 2, reuse all three slides from **p4G_Jury_Qualifications**.

Insert a footer on all slides except the title slide that displays the text **Presented by Firstname Lastname** On the Notes and Handouts, insert a header that displays the text **Paralegal Training** a footer that displays the file name **Lastname Firstname 4G Jury Selection** a date that updates automatically, and the page number.

Modify the presentation as follows:

1 On Slide 1, change the font in the title placeholder to 48 pt bold, and then center the text in the placeholder. Apply bold and shadow font effects to the subtitle text and center align in the placeholder. Apply Bottom Align paragraph setting to the text in the subtitle placeholder.

2 On Slide 2, move the title placeholder up about a half inch on the slide, and then apply bold and Blue-Gray, Accent 1, Darker 25% font color to the text. Convert the three lines of bulleted text to the Process Funnel SmartArt graphic. In the Text pane, enter a fourth line of text **Jury Pool** Resize the SmartArt graphic to 4.8" high by 7" wide. Apply the 3-D Cartoon style to the SmartArt, and then change colors to Colorful Range – Accent Colors 4 to 5. Center the SmartArt graphic on the slide. In the Notes pane, type the text **Process used in Colorado. Other states may differ.**

3 Use Format Painter to apply the font effects of the title text on Slide 2 to the title text on all slides after it except the last slide. Move the title text placeholder up about a half inch on Slides 3 through 10.

4 On Slide 3, convert the bulleted text to a Vertical Curved List SmartArt graphic. Size the graphic to 5" high by 7.41" wide. Change the graphic colors to Colorful Range – Accent Colors 4 to 5, and then apply the 3-D Cartoon style. Reposition the graphic to the center of the slide.

5 On Slide 4, size the SmartArt graphic to 5" high by 7.41" wide. Change the graphic colors to Colorful Range – Accent Colors 4 to 5, and then apply the 3-D Cartoon style. Reposition the graphic to the center of the slide. In the Notes pane, type the source of your information **http://www.courts.state.co.us/Jury/Index.cfm**

6 On Slide 5, size the SmartArt graphic to 4.5" high by 7.41" wide. Change the graphic colors to Colorful Range – Accent Colors 4 to 5, and then apply the 3-D Sunset Scene style. Reposition the graphic to the center of the slide. Animate the SmartArt with a Fly In Entrance, and then set Effect Options to From Top Right that displays using a One by One sequence. Use the Animation Painter to apply this animation effect to the SmartArt graphic on Slide 2.

7 On Slide 6, change the slide layout to a Two Content layout. Apply WordArt Gradient Fill - Blue-Gray, Accent 1 to the title text, and if necessary, reduce the font size until the text fits on one line. In the right placeholder, insert the **p4G_Jury.wmf** picture. Size the picture to 2.4" high by 3.5" wide, and then apply the picture style Center Shadow Rectangle. Position the picture as shown in Figure 4. Insert a text box below the picture, and then type **www.websters-online-dictionary.org** in the text box. Inside the text box, change the font size to 16 pt, and then adjust the size of the text box if necessary so that the text fits on one line and is centered. Apply Shape Style Intense Effect - Teal, Accent 5 to the text box. Arrange the picture and the text box to be center aligned.

(Project 4G Jury Selection continues on the next page)

GO! Make It | Project **4G** Jury Selection (continued)

8 On Slide 7, format the background by applying **p4G_Courtroom** as a picture fill. Hide the background graphics. To the left placeholder, apply Shape Fill Brown, Accent 3, Lighter 40%, and then to the right placeholder, apply Shape Fill Teal, Accent 5, Lighter 60%. Resize both placeholders to 2.97" high by 4.5" wide, and then reposition them at the bottom corners of the slide. To the title placeholder, apply Shape Fill Tan, Accent 2, Lighter 40%. Resize the title placeholder to .9" high by 10" wide and position at the top of the slide. Center the text in the title placeholder. Remove the footer from the slide.

9 On Slide 8, select the existing table, and then apply Table Style Themed Style 1 – Accent 2. Size the table to 4.5" high by 8" wide, and then position it in the center of the slide. In the top row, center the text, and then change the font size to 24 pt. In the bottom row, center the text. In the remaining rows, change the font size to 18 pt. Remove the footer from the slide.

10 On Slide 9, create a 3-D Clustered Column chart, and then type the data below in the chart. Delete unused Category 4 row and Series 3 columns in Excel. Apply Chart Layout 3 and Chart Style 18, and then type **Nationwide** for the title. Size the chart to 4.5" high by 8" wide, and then position the chart in the center of the slide.

	Jury Trials	Bench Trials
Total Trials	18,404	8,513
Plaintiff Winners	10,012	5,809
Plaintiff Winners $1M or More	1,159	137

11 On Slide 10, change the layout of the slide to Picture with Caption. Insert the picture **p4G_Federal_Court**. Animate the objects on the slide with the Shape entrance. Change the Effect Options to Diamond. Reorder the animation if necessary so that the picture displays first, the *Closing Thoughts* text displays second, and the quotation with author displays third.

12 Apply the Doors transition to all slides.

13 Run the slide show and proofread. Change the print settings so that the presentation is printed as Handouts (3 slides per page). Save the presentation and submit it as directed.

End **You have completed Project 4G** ——————————————

Paralegal

GO! Think | Project 4H Community Presentation

Project Files

For Project 4H, you will need the following file:

New blank PowerPoint presentation

You will save your presentation as:

Lastname_Firstname_4H_Community_Presentation

Save your file in your Paralegal folder with the name **Lastname_Firstname_4H_Community_Presentation**

Your local paralegal professional organization does community service workshops on legal topics. Many legal procedures can be completed by individual citizens because the information is now available on the Internet. You have volunteered to create the presentation for next month.

Research the Internet for your state, city, and/or district and county to find information related to a topic that you think would be of interest to those in your local community. Go to the following Web site to get started:

http://www.ncsconline.org/D_kis/info_court_web_sites.html

Examples could include information about Appointment of a Guardian, Appointment of a Conservator, Bankruptcy, Estates, Evictions, Victim Restitution, Probate, or Small Claims.

Include instructions on filing, common term information, fees, forms and where to find them, statistics, and any other pertinent information related to your topic. You may also want to talk about the court structure of your state. Keep in mind that your presentation is to summarize the information about the topic. You should cite your source(s) in your presentation.

1. Apply an appropriate theme and theme color.

2. Apply a background style.

3. Keep bulleted slides to a maximum of two. Customize the bullets on the bulleted slides. Follow the 6×6 rule. (No more than 6 lines of text and no more than 6 words in a line.)

4. Use SmartArt on at least three slides. Animate the SmartArt on these slides.

5. Use at least one table OR chart and apply animation.

6. Use clip art or a photo on at least two slides. Apply a picture style and picture effects. Animate the clip art or photos.

7. Use WordArt on at least one slide.

8. Use drawing objects on at least one slide. Add text to the drawing objects. Animate the objects.

9. Insert notes in the Notes pane of points you plan to make during the presentation.

10. Apply slide transitions.

11. Insert a header and footer for the Notes and Handouts. Include the date and have it automatically update. Add the page number and filename **Lastname_Firstname_4H_Community_Presentation** to the footer. Insert the slide number on each slide, but do not include it on the title slide.

12. Run the slide show and proofread. Change the print settings so the presentation is printed as Notes Pages. Save the presentation and submit it as directed.

End You have completed Project 4H —————————

Index

SINGLE PC LICENSE AGREEMENT AND LIMITED WARRANTY

READ THIS LICENSE CAREFULLY BEFORE OPENING THIS PACKAGE. BY OPENING THIS PACKAGE, YOU ARE AGREEING TO THE TERMS AND CONDITIONS OF THIS LICENSE. IF YOU DO NOT AGREE, DO NOT OPEN THE PACKAGE. PROMPTLY RETURN THE UNOPENED PACKAGE AND ALL ACCOMPANYING ITEMS TO THE PLACE YOU OBTAINED THEM. *THESE TERMS APPLY TO ALL LICENSED SOFTWARE ON THE DISK EXCEPT THAT THE TERMS FOR USE OF ANY SHAREWARE OR FREEWARE ON THE DISKETTES ARE AS SET FORTH IN THE ELECTRONIC LICENSE LOCATED ON THE DISK:*

1. GRANT OF LICENSE and OWNERSHIP: The enclosed computer programs ("Software") are licensed, not sold, to you by Prentice-Hall, Inc. ("We" or the "Company") and in consideration of your purchase or adoption of the accompanying Company textbooks and/or other materials, and your agreement to these terms. We reserve any rights not granted to you. You own only the disk(s) but we and/or our licensors own the Software itself. This license allows you to use and display your copy of the Software on a single computer (i.e., with a single CPU) at a single location for academic use only, so long as you comply with the terms of this Agreement. You may make one copy for back up, or transfer your copy to another CPU, provided that the Software is usable on only one computer.

2. RESTRICTIONS: You may not transfer or distribute the Software or documentation to anyone else. Except for backup, you may not copy the documentation or the Software. You may not network the Software or otherwise use it on more than one computer or computer terminal at the same time. You may not reverse engineer, disassemble, decompile, modify, adapt, translate, or create derivative works based on the Software or the Documentation. You may be held legally responsible for any copying or copyright infringement which is caused by your failure to abide by the terms of these restrictions.

3. TERMINATION: This license is effective until terminated. This license will terminate automatically without notice from the Company if you fail to comply with any provisions or limitations of this license. Upon termination, you shall destroy the Documentation and all copies of the Software. All provisions of this Agreement as to limitation and disclaimer of warranties, limitation of liability, remedies or damages, and our ownership rights shall survive termination.

4. DISCLAIMER OF WARRANTY: THE COMPANY AND ITS LICENSORS MAKE NO WARRANTIES ABOUT THE SOFTWARE, WHICH IS PROVIDED "AS-IS." IF THE DISK IS DEFECTIVE IN MATERIALS OR WORKMANSHIP, YOUR ONLY REMEDY IS TO RETURN IT TO THE COMPANY WITHIN 30 DAYS FOR REPLACEMENT UNLESS THE COMPANY DETERMINES IN GOOD FAITH THAT THE DISK HAS BEEN MISUSED OR IMPROPERLY INSTALLED, REPAIRED, ALTERED OR DAMAGED. THE COMPANY DISCLAIMS ALL WARRANTIES, EXPRESS OR IMPLIED, INCLUDING WITHOUT LIMITATION, THE IMPLIED WARRANTIES OF MERCHANTABILITY AND FITNESS FOR A PARTICULAR PURPOSE. THE COMPANY DOES NOT WARRANT, GUARANTEE OR MAKE ANY REPRESENTATION REGARDING THE ACCURACY, RELIABILITY, CURRENTNESS, USE, OR RESULTS OF USE, OF THE SOFTWARE.

5. LIMITATION OF REMEDIES AND DAMAGES: IN NO EVENT, SHALL THE COMPANY OR ITS EMPLOYEES, AGENTS, LICENSORS OR CONTRACTORS BE LIABLE FOR ANY INCIDENTAL, INDIRECT, SPECIAL OR CONSEQUENTIAL DAMAGES ARISING OUT OF OR IN CONNECTION WITH THIS LICENSE OR THE SOFTWARE, INCLUDING, WITHOUT LIMITATION, LOSS OF USE, LOSS OF DATA, LOSS OF INCOME OR PROFIT, OR OTHER LOSSES SUSTAINED AS A RESULT OF INJURY TO ANY PERSON, OR LOSS OF OR DAMAGE TO PROPERTY, OR CLAIMS OF THIRD PARTIES, EVEN IF THE COMPANY OR AN AUTHORIZED REPRESENTATIVE OF THE COMPANY HAS BEEN ADVISED OF THE POSSIBILITY OF SUCH DAMAGES. SOME JURISDICTIONS DO NOT ALLOW THE LIMITATION OF DAMAGES IN CERTAIN CIRCUMSTANCES, SO THE ABOVE LIMITATIONS MAY NOT ALWAYS APPLY.

6. GENERAL: THIS AGREEMENT SHALL BE CONSTRUED IN ACCORDANCE WITH THE LAWS OF THE UNITED STATES OF AMERICA AND THE STATE OF NEW YORK, APPLICABLE TO CONTRACTS MADE IN NEW YORK, AND SHALL BENEFIT THE COMPANY, ITS AFFILIATES AND ASSIGNEES. This Agreement is the complete and exclusive statement of the agreement between you and the Company and supersedes all proposals, prior agreements, oral or written, and any other communications between you and the company or any of its representatives relating to the subject matter. If you are a U.S. Government user, this Software is licensed with "restricted rights" as set forth in subparagraphs (a)-(d) of the Commercial Computer-Restricted Rights clause at FAR 52.227-19 or in subparagraphs (c)(1)(ii) of the Rights in Technical Data and Computer Software clause at DFARS 252.227-7013, and similar clauses, as applicable.

Should you have any questions concerning this agreement or if you wish to contact the Company for any reason, please contact in writing:

Multimedia Production,
Higher Education Division,
Prentice-Hall, Inc.,
1 Lake Street,
Upper Saddle River NJ 07458.